Ethical Decision Making and Information Technology

ABOUT THE AUTHORS

Ernest A. Kallman is Professor of Computer Information Systems at Bentley College and a Research Fellow at the Bentley Center for Business Ethics. He coordinates the MIS course and also teaches systems analysis and design, I/S management, and I/S policy. Ernie holds a B.S. degree in Economics from St. Peters College, an M.B.A. from Baruch College, and a Ph.D. in Management Planning Systems from the City University of New York. Prior to entering academia he spent twelve years in the computer industry, where, among other positions, he was an officer and director of a software firm and a director of a mini-computer company.

Ernie has authored three books and numerous articles about the management of the information systems function, recently concentrating on ethical issues and privacy concerns. He is currently conducting a major research project on how organizations protect confidential information. He is also a consultant to organizations seeking to develop privacy policies and ethics training programs. At Bentley he is on a college-wide task force responsible for fostering ethics education across the curriculum.

John P. Grillo is Professor of Computer Information Systems at Bentley College and a Research Fellow at the Bentley Center for Business Ethics. He is coordinator of the introductory computer course and the department's Security and Privacy course, a popular elective offered at both the undergraduate and graduate levels.

At the University of New Mexico, John earned a Ph.D. in Educational Research, majoring in Computer Science. Before joining Bentley in 1979, he taught at the University of New Mexico, West Texas State University, and Western Illinois University.

John has co-authored (with J. D. Robertson, also of Bentley) fourteen texts and professional books in the areas of personal computer programming, graphics, and data structures. His present specialty is computer security and privacy, which initiated his interest in ethics.

Ethical Decision Making and Information Technology

An Introduction with Cases
2nd Edition

Ernest A. Kallman
Bentley College

John P. Grillo
Bentley College

The McGraw-Hill Companies, Inc.

New York St. Louis San Francisco Auckland Bogotá
Caracas Lisbon London Madrid Mexico Milan Montreal
New Delhi San Juan Singapore Sydney Tokyo Toronto

To our wives, for their love and support . . .
Sandy and Betsy

McGraw-Hill
A Division of The **McGraw·Hill** Companies

Ethical Decision Making and Information Technology
An Introduction with Cases, Second Edition

1 2 3 4 5 6 7 8 9 0 FGR FGR 9 0 9 8 7 6 5

ISB 0-07-034090-0

Sponsoring editor: *Frank Ruggirello*
Editorial assistant: *Kyle Thomes*
Production supervisor: *Richard DeVitto*
Project manager: *Fritz/Brett Associates*
Cover design: *Michael Rogondino*
Interior design: *Rogondino & Associates*
Compositor: *Pat Rogondino*
Printer and binder: *Quebecor Printing Fairfield, Inc.*

Library of Congress Catalog Card Number 95-78226

CONTENTS

Appendix A: Ethics Codes and Policies   109

Appendix B: Worksheets for the Four-Step Analysis Process   121

PREFACE TO
THE INSTRUCTOR

Today we are used to hearing stories about the unethical use of information technology (IT): violations of data confidentiality, software piracy, and computer viruses are primary examples. Every day IT offers us new opportunities to compete more effectively. At the same time, the misuse of technology clearly has increased the threat to individuals and organizations from financial loss, tarnished reputations, and legal action.

Ethical Decision Making and Information Technology: An Introduction with Cases, Second Edition, is designed to challenge that threat. It is designed for use as a supplement for any information systems or computer science course that shares our commitment to teaching students how to recognize, evaluate, and react responsibly to ethical dilemmas, and how to behave ethically themselves.

Building a Conceptual Foundation

This text assumes no prerequisites. Chapter 1 defines ethics and introduces an ethical decision-making process. Chapter 2 relates ethics to IT. Chapter 3 applies a four-step analysis process to a real-world ethical dilemma involving IT, illustrating how to reach defensible ethical decisions. These introductory chapters equip students to evaluate the 19 real-world cases in Part II intelligently and systematically.

The Cases

The 19 cases in this book have been developed over four years and class-tested by dozens of information systems and computer science instructors, most of them new to teaching ethics. They are based on actual situations; only the names of the people and organizations have been changed. Dialogue has been included to enhance the realism of the case. The cases provide a blend of essential and nonessential facts that challenge students to separate "the wheat from the chaff," one of the fundamental skills developed by *Ethical Decision Making and Information Technology,* Second Edition.

To offer instructors flexibility, the cases cover a variety of topics. The table that follows delineates the 19 cases according to major ethical issues and appropriate course use. The accompanying *Instructor's Manual* includes guidelines for customizing the cases to be consistent with specific course objectives.

CASE MATRIX

Case	Title	Topics	Courses
1	Levity or Libel?	Misuse of company resources Accountability for actions	Data Communications Office Automation MIS Intro. to IS
2	Credit Woes	Accuracy Vendor/client conflicts Credit bureaus	Database MIS Intro. to IS
3,3A	Something for Everyone	Privacy Data recombination	Data Structures Database MIS Intro. to IS
4	Abort, Retry, Ignore	Unauthorized access Whistle blowing Data access	Operating Systems Security and Privacy MIS Intro. to IS
5	Messages from All Over	Inappropriate use of resources E-mail Surveillance Privacy	Data Communications Policy Network Management MIS Intro. to IS
6	A Job on the Side	Duty Consulting responsibilities Respect	Systems Analysis System Design MIS Intro. to IS
7,7A	The New Job	Inappropriate use of resources Offensive graphic image Sexual harassment	Small Business Systems MIS Intro. to IS
8	The Buyout	Privacy Data Access	Security and Privacy Policy MIS Intro. to IS
9	Charades	Password theft Misuse of authority and power Lack of respect Duty	Security and Privacy Operating Systems MIS Intro. to IS
10	Laccaria and Eagle	Gray market International trade Protectionist measures Consistency	Policy Small Bus. Systems MIS Intro. to IS

Case	Title	Topics	Courses
11	Taking Bad with Good	Premature software release Unprofessional behavior Virus released in retribution	Systems Design Policy Data Communications MIS Intro. to IS
12	The Engineer and the Teacher	Power in society Poor school vs. rich eng. firm Software piracy Consistency	Intro. to Computers Security and Privacy MIS Intro. to IS
13	Test Data	Ethics of development Breaking trust Keeping quiet Privacy	Systems Analysis System Design MIS Intro. to IS
14	The Brain Pick	Knowledge engineering Expert Systems	Artificial Intelligence Expert Systems MIS Intro. to IS
15	Trouble in Sardonia	Copyrights International policy Consistency	Policy Security and Privacy MIS Intro. to IS
16	Bad Medicine	Ethical impact study Computer crime Arrogance of IS professionals	System Design Policy Security and Privacy Network Management MIS Intro. to IS
17	Code Blue	Privacy Technical limitations	Systems Analysis System Design Policy MIS Intro. to IS
18	Virtual Success	Virtual reality The "dark side" Expert systems Artificial intelligence	Artificial Intelligence Virtual Reality MIS Intro. to IS
19	His Private Lab	Consistency Misuse of resources Rights and duties	Policy MIS Intro. to IS

Distinguishing Features

■ **Assumes No Prerequisites:** Part I equips students with a conceptual foundation designed to help them recognize, evaluate, and react responsibly to the ethical dilemmas in each case study.

■ **Flexible:** Supplements any information systems or computer science text. While providing sufficient detail for robust analysis, each two-page case can be discussed within a single class period. Instructors can mix and match the cases most appropriate to their specific course objectives.

■ **Real World:** The 19 cases are based on actual events. They raise a variety of ethical dilemmas, and can be used in the courses as illustrated in the Case Matrix.

■ **Case Worksheet:** A set of case worksheets are provided that lead the student through the four-step analysis and decision-making process. The worksheet organizes student responses and provides a basis for class discussion and grading.

■ **Comprehensive Instructor's Manual:** Written with instructors new to teaching ethics in mind, this manual includes: How to Use the Text, Guidelines for Assigning and Evaluating Cases, Strategies for Managing Classroom Discussion, Case Objectives, Key Ethical Issues, Case Discussion Ideas, and Exam Questions.

Revisions to the Second Edition

The essential elements of the first edition have not been altered. This second edition reflects necessary refinements uncovered through our own classroom use and that of others who have been kind enough to report back. We have expanded explanations and resequenced some sections. The two major revisions are the expanded explanations and analyses in Chapter 3 and the completely new worksheet. The *Instructor's Manual* has been thoroughly updated.

Chapter 1

■ The entire discussion of laws, guidelines, and principles has been reorganized. Approaches to Ethical Decision Making, Figure 1-1, has been revised.

■ The relationship between law and ethics is discussed at length, but the point is clearly made that at some point the two diverge and ethical decision making must move on without the law.

■ Guidelines, an important part of ethical analysis, are deemphasized in the sense that the ethical analysis doesn't end with the guidelines.

- Lead-in questions have been added to facilitate the application of the informal guidelines.

- The Rights and Duties section has been expanded to make clearer the relationship between the two. Diagrams and numerous examples have been added.

- A discussion of altruism has been added to the Consequentialism section.

- All references have been updated and annotated.

Chapter 2

- The Internet has been added in the Social and Economics Issues section, the E-Mail Issues section, and the Resource Exploitation Issues section.

- The E-Mail Issues section has been rewritten extensively to reflect current practice.

Chapter 3

- The sample case analysis is completely revised to reflect the new decision-making worksheet.

- The sample case commentary is restructured into three distinct sections:
  - An explanation of the decision-making process
  - The author's solution
  - An explanation of how that solution was derived

Worksheet

- The revised worksheet reflects major improvements in the four-step decision-making process.
  a. The sequence of tasks has been altered to logically separate the ultimate ethical issue from other problems in the case.
  b. Instructions have been revised to clarify what is expected in a particular response.
  c. Analysis of legal issues has been moved to be earlier in the analysis.
  d. The worksheet space for applying ethical principles has been expanded since this is where the true analysis takes place.

- Step 3, the resolution section, has been revised to guide students through how a solution must be implemented.

- Ensuring the rights of the stakeholders has been made a specific part of the resolution section.
- Pivot point analysis (How and when could this have been avoided?) is now a formal part of the resolution section.

The Cases

- Three cases—3, 7, and 19—are now in role-playing format.
- A new case, 19, focuses on inappropriate use of organizational resources.
- All cases were revised to remove English-language idioms in order to make the cases useful to people for whom English is not their first language.
- Two cases now include the Internet as part of the situation.
- All cases are revised to sharpen the focus of the ethical dilemma.

Ethics Codes and Policies

This new section contains an explanation of professional codes and organizational policies. The ACM Code of Conduct as well as sample organizational codes and policies for ethical computer use, e-mail privacy, and Internet use are included.

Instructor's Manual

- There is a new section with sample exam questions.
- An expanded classroom management section explains new techniques such as role-playing cases.
- There is revised commentary on every case that defines the ethical dilemma and explains possible discussion options.
- There are revised references and sources for help.

A Final Comment

By emphasizing the need for information systems professionals and users to behave ethically, we do not want to imply that these individuals are less ethical than those in any other profession. Although the cases included in this book often depict people who are committing inappropriate acts, in reality such actions are performed by a small percentage of users of IT. And, as we remind students, *most of the unethical activity that does occur has occurred because individuals did not realize an act was unethical, or did not know how to make ethical decisions.*

Acknowledgments

A special thanks to the graduate students in the Bentley College MSCIS program who, through their personal and professional experiences, discovered the ethical situations upon which most of the cases in this book are based. For their sensitivity to ethical situations and their commitment to ethical computer use, we congratulate them. We thank them all for their willingness to share their episodes. We're sorry we could include so few.

To the Bentley CIS faculty who were so candid in their feedback and so willing to try new things, we are deeply grateful.

And also some heartfelt thanks to those who attended our Teaching Ethics seminars and shared your needs, fears, and ambitions, as well as those who responded to our invitation to send along your comments and critiques. We are especially appreciative for all the help on internationalizing that we received from Robert Davison in Hong Kong. We hope this new edition shows that we heard you.

Thanks also to our copy editor, Susan Defosset, who seemed to know what we wanted to say and made it happen, and to Elaine Brett whose cheerful creativity solved many a formatting dilemma.

Additional thanks are due to the following for their advice and counsel:

Eli Cohen, Wichita State University
Brett Ellis, BYU-Hawaii
Thomas Hilton, Utah State
Roy Johnson, Idaho State
Donald Schaupp, Southern Wesleyan University

Finally, a special tribute to Linda Cotroneo of the CIS Department staff, who always stood ready to cheerfully pick up the loose ends and the occasional pieces that were falling through the cracks.

Free Diskette Available

A diskette of exam questions and transparency masters is available from the authors. Please tell us something about the course in which you are using the book and include your full postal mailing address. We also urge you to send us your comments, critiques, and ideas as you use the book and *Instructor's Manual*. We'll use them, as we did for this second edition, to make the book and the *Instructor's Manual* better.

Ernest Kallman
ekallman@bentley.edu

John Grillo
jgrillo@bentley.edu

Bentley College
Waltham, MA 02154-4705

1

Approaches to Ethical Decision Making

The objectives of the chapters in Part 1 are to:

■ Raise sensitivity to ethical circumstances involving information technology—circumstances that have the potential to harm individuals, organizations, or society.

■ Provide a process for analyzing ethical situations and for making decisions in response to them.

■ Instill in each reader a readiness and a willingness to accept responsibility for the ethicality of his or her actions.

Chapter

1

Ethics and Ethical Decision Making

WHY WE SHOULD CARE ABOUT ETHICS

Ethics has to do with making a principle-based choice between competing alternatives. In the simplest ethical dilemmas, this choice is between right and wrong. Ethical dilemmas occur in business as well as in our personal lives. We hear about them on TV, on the job, and in school, and we read about them in the popular press. More and more, the ethical situations involve technology, particularly information technology, a field that includes computers, telecommunications, and video.

When the situation involves us personally, we can often influence its resolution. But to exercise positive influence, we must understand both the nature of the problem and how to analyze it. The easy part is understanding the problem. Even in situations involving computers, this does not necessarily mean knowing a great deal about technology. The more difficult task is attacking the problem logically and making decisions based on well-reasoned, defensible *ethical principles*.

For a responsible person, ethical principles are an essential part of solving the problem. Ethical principles are ideas of behavior that are commonly acceptable to society. Using ethical principles as a basis for decision making prevents us from relying only on intuition or personal preference.

Why should we care about ethics? The number of ethical choices we face every day makes it imperative that we care. Obviously, some unethical actions—even if made unwittingly—can put us on the wrong side of the law. Other unethical actions, though not illegal, can have drastic consequences

3

for our careers and reputations. Therefore, each of us must care about ethical behavior as a matter of self-interest. Knowing the principles of ethical decision making is a cultural survival skill. In addition, each person who benefits from living in society has an obligation to uphold the principles on which that society is based. Therefore, ethical decision making is vital to creating a world in which we want to live.

This chapter will explain what ethics has to do with information technology, how ethics relates to human action, how to choose between right and wrong, how to choose between two "rights," where laws come in, and how to use a number of guidelines and ethical principles to make ethical decisions.

COMPUTER ETHICS AND REGULAR ETHICS

Is "computer ethics," or ethics regarding information technology, really different from "regular" ethics? Is there an ethical difference between browsing through someone else's computer file and browsing through her desk drawer? Most experts agree that there is actually no special category of computer ethics; rather, there are ethical situations in which computers are involved. The capabilities of the computer often lend a special character to problems of computer ethics, however. For instance, the computer often allows people to perform unethical actions faster or to perform actions that were too difficult or impossible using manual methods. Now that computers are so common, organizations and individuals are increasingly vulnerable to their unethical use.

Some people do browse through computer files when they are not authorized to do so. And some people who use computers and who develop systems for computers perform numerous other unethical and illegal activities. Activities such as violation of copyright and invasion of privacy threaten to harm both individuals and organizations. The problem will get worse as the number of computers increases, as more people use them, and as the computers assume more critical roles in the organizations that use them.

Another characteristic common to computer ethics is the difficulty of identifying ethical issues. Many of those who perform practices with computers that others perceive as unethical do not see the ethical implications of their behavior. Their first reaction when caught is, "I didn't know I did anything wrong. I only looked at the file. I didn't take it." If they copy a file, they say, "I didn't do anything wrong. The file is still there for the owner. I just made a copy." Hackers often say, "I was just testing to see how secure the system was. I was going to report the weakness to management. I was performing a valuable service." One of the major objectives of this book is to increase your sensitivity to ethical issues involving computers so that you will recognize the issues when you see them. (This is, in fact, the purpose of Chapter 2.)

As later sections of this chapter will discuss, a third characteristic of computer ethics is the wide array of ethical dilemmas the computer presents. The computer user and developer are routinely faced with a range of ethical options from simply not nice to blatantly illegal.

Computer ethics should have a strong link to policy or strategy. Once an ethical problem is identified, a policy or strategy should be developed to prevent the problem from recurring or to deal with it if it does.

COMPETING FACTORS THAT AFFECT OUR BEHAVIOR

At the biological level, behavior is directed by the drives for food, shelter, and love. At the societal level, we behave according to a variety of rules that flow from government, religious institutions or the family. At a higher and more abstract level, our behavior is modified by our understanding of what is good, right, proper, moral, or *ethical*.

Human action is rarely simple or straightforward. At any given time, influences from several levels affect our behavior. These influences often lead to competing outcomes, so an individual must weigh risks and consequences before making an independent value judgment about how to act.

Decisions involving information technology incorporate as many levels as other decisions. In addition to involving personal needs and desires and public values, decisions about computer technology typically involve many shades of gray—possibilities that, by social standards, are not exclusively right or wrong.

VALUE JUDGMENTS

Value judgments are at the heart of personal or business decisions in which ethics has a bearing on the choice to be made. The objective is to make a judgment, based on a combination of your values and those of others, to arrive at a defensible principled choice. The risk in applying ethical values is poor judgment. Poor judgment, or a low-quality decision, can result from inadequate examination of the facts, failure to apply appropriate ethical principles, or failure to consider all perspectives of an issue. A low-quality decision can have a wide range of results: It can hurt a person's feelings, lower employee morale, cause a business to lose customers, decrease profits, or cause a firm to be sued or go bankrupt. In addition, poor judgment can have negative effects for society—by destroying confidence in public officials, for example. One way to achieve a high-quality ethical value judgment is through a structured-analysis and decision-making process such as described in Chapter 3.

THE TWO TYPES OF ETHICAL CHOICES

One type of ethical choice involves choosing right from wrong. The other type involves choosing right from right.

Choosing Right from Wrong

Most of us agree that stealing, lying, and cheating are wrong. These three actions are the taboos of a common-sense morality. For instance, if we take the hotel towels, we know we are stealing and that the act is wrong. If we swear to the judge that we were going 55 miles per hour when we were actually going 75, we know we are lying and that the act is wrong. If we use someone else's answers on an exam, we know we are cheating and that the act is wrong. You can probably describe half a dozen such situations in as many minutes.

Choosing Right from Right

Ethical choices become more difficult when the situation is not as clear, is not black or white, but contains some shades of gray. Is it wrong to steal food if you are starving? Is it wrong if your child is starving? Is it wrong to keep any coins you find in a pay telephone? Does the money belong to the previous caller? To the phone company? To you? Does the amount make a difference? (Keep a small amount, return a large amount?) How would you return the coins? Do you call the operator and offer to feed the coins back into the machine? What if the operator will not take them? Are you off the hook, so to speak? Should you give all the money to charity?

Lying may be wrong, but when we visit a sick friend, is it wrong to exaggerate how well he or she looks? We may be lying about our friend's condition, but we are probably doing it to achieve what we perceive to be a higher good: the quick recovery or general welfare of the patient. Cheating is wrong, but are we cheating at poker when we steal a look at someone's cards when we're only playing for matches?

These examples, however trivial, are typical of the structure of many ethical situations. They illustrate the complexity of *ethical choice*—the necessity to choose a course of action from two or more alternatives, each having some desirable result. In other words, in an ethical choice, an individual often must choose between two or more "goods," or the lesser of two "evils," or between two or more paths to achieve some desirable objective. These choices are often influenced by many factors of varying degrees of relevance.

To explore the problem of choosing among alternatives that are neither wholly right nor wholly wrong, consider the following ethical dilemmas:

- How much security do we impose on computer files? When we make sign-on procedures easier and encourage system use, do we leave certain data files vulnerable to browsing (which may invade the privacy of some employees or clients and cause them harm)? Or do we protect the data better and lose those users (or customers) who will not bother to wade through the tighter controls? In other words, is the objective user friendliness or data protection? How much user friendliness are we willing to sacrifice for data protection, or how much risk to data confidentiality are we willing to take to foster user friendliness? This is a choice between two goods.

- New software is promised, and sorely needed, by a specific date. The project is late. Do we install software that is not fully tested? If so, do we inform the client or user? Do we install software with less functionality than promised? If so, do we inform the client or user? Do we "bust the budget" and work overtime to meet the deadline? Do we ask for an extension? In this case, the worthwhile objective of meeting the deadline has more than one path to its achievement.

These kinds of ethical situations, which include competing interests, each with some merit, are the most difficult to handle. Even after the ethical choice is made, we may have to make an additional effort to convince those on the other side that the choice was the best for all concerned.

MAKING DEFENSIBLE DECISIONS

Discovering Ethical Dilemmas

The first step in ethical decision making is to recognize that an ethical dilemma exists and that an ethical decision is called for. This is often not easy, particularly where computers are concerned. Furthermore, when an ethical dilemma is discovered, it may be just a vague feeling or an ill-defined set of circumstances. Help is needed to clarify the action in question and to articulate it. Only when the ethical issue is clear can meaningful analysis and decision making take place.

All of us address ethical decisions with some sense of right and wrong acquired in our upbringing. But many, especially young people, have had few opportunities to test their convictions. They may never have had to make the hard choice between taking the consequences of their convictions or avoiding the issue. They may never have had to choose between giving up a good job and acting ethically, or agreeing to perform some unethical act to keep a job. They may never have had to wrestle with what to do when they discovered that someone was acting unethically. For this reason, it is important to learn how to evaluate ethical situations and make defensible decisions.

Notice that the phrase used is "defensible decisions," not "right decisions." Two well-meaning individuals can examine the same ethical situation and arrive at different courses of action. A high-quality ethical decision is based on reason and can be defended according to ethical concepts. By applying one or more ethical concepts to a situation, a person can rationally examine alternative options and choose the best one. Another person may apply other ethical principles and defend a different "best" option. Such dual (or multiple) solutions to one ethical dilemma point out how differing value judgments impact ethical decision making.

Making ethical decisions is by no means a science. People approach it differently. In one sense, ethical questions could be answered with that most ubiquitous of responses: It all depends. But in ethical decision making, the individual must decide what the answer does depend on: what the facts are, the consequences of each alternative, and which course is most beneficial. The next sections will discuss how laws, guidelines, and ethical principles all contribute to discovering ethical dilemmas and making ethical choices. Figure 1-1 summarizes these approaches.

Law and Ethics

When a law tells us to do or not to do something, it implies that a recognized authority has decided that the action the law allows or prohibits is of benefit to society in some way. You may ask, "What was the basis for any decision regarding this issue before this law was written?" It often happens that an ethical principle was used prior to a law's construction. As you recall, ethical principles are ideas of behavior that are commonly acceptable to society.

For example, the generally accepted ethical principle that we should help others in need leads to specific Good Samaritan laws that protect the rights of individuals who help an injured person. In the computer field, the principle of recognizing an individual's right to ownership of an original work and to a fair economic return has led to copyright laws that protect software.

The fact that law is grounded in ethical principles makes law a good starting point for ethical decision making. In other words, when we are confronted with an ethical decision, we should first research the law. In some instances, the law will clearly apply and lead directly to the appropriate ethical conclusion. However, in many situations, the law will not provide a straightforward solution. There are bad laws, and there are times when individuals may ethically choose to disobey the law. The relationship between ethics and law leads to four possible states that depend on whether a specific act is ethical or not ethical (unethical), and legal or not legal (illegal). Table 1-1 presents these states visually.

Table 1-1 Legality versus Ethicality

	Legal	Not Legal
Ethical	I	II
Not Ethical	III	IV

I = An act that is ethical and legal
II = An act that is ethical but not legal
III = An act that is not ethical but is legal
IV = An act that is not ethical and not legal

Source: Wagner, Jennifer L. (1991).

Figure 3-1
Approaches to Ethical Decision Making

Law and Ethics

Does the law provide an answer? (Professional help should be sought.)

Guidelines

Informal Guidelines

1. Is there something you or others would prefer to keep quiet?
>   Are there "shushers" in the situation? Who wants to keep things quiet?
>   Does it pass the Mom Test: Would you tell her? Would she do it?
>   Does it pass the TV Test: Would you tell a nationwide audience?
>   Does it pass the Market Test: Could you advertise the activity to gain a market edge?

2. Does your instinct tell you that something is wrong?
>   Does it pass the Smell Test: Does the situation "smell"?

Formal Guidelines

1. Does the act violate corporate policy?
2. Does the act violate corporate or professional codes of conduct or ethics?
3. Does the act violate the Golden Rule?

Ethical Principles

Rights and Duties (deontology)

Are any rights abridged?
>   The right to know
>   The right to privacy
>   The right to property

Are any duties or responsibilities not met?

Personal duties:
- Trust
- Integrity
- Truthfulness
- Gratitude and reparation
- Justice
- Beneficence and nonmaleficence
- Self-improvement

Professional duties (responsibilities)
>   For all professionals:
>   Maintain appropriate professional relationships
>   Maintain efficacy
>   For information professionals in particular:
>   Maintain confidentiality
>   Maintain impartiality

Consequentialism (teleology)

Does the action minimize actual and potential harm?

>   Egoism: good for me, least harm to me
>   Utilitarianism: good for the group, least harm for the group
>   Altruism: good for all, some harm to me

Kant's Categorical Imperative

The principle of consistency: What if everyone acted this way?
The principle of respect: Are people treated as ends rather than means?

The outline that follows presents examples of actions that might fit in each category in the preceding table. Note that the categorization of an action depends on a given set of laws and value judgments, offering much room for disagreement.

I. Ethical and legal

- Firing an individual who does not perform according to expectations or who fails to follow certain contractual obligations
- Increasing the price of goods to reflect new material cost increases
- Buying a software package to do accounting for clients

II. Ethical but not legal

- Copying copyrighted software to use only as a backup, even when the copyright agreement specifically prohibits copying for that purpose
- Using civil disobedience to attract attention to a "just" cause

III. Not ethical but legal

- Revealing data that was expected to remain confidential—for example, by data entry operators gossiping about the salary data they are processing
- Not citing sources in a research paper
- Using an unlicensed copy of Lotus 1-2-3 in a foreign country that has no software copyright laws
- Distributing mailing lists or other legally obtained personal information without the knowledge of the people on the lists

IV. Not ethical and not legal

- Making unauthorized copies of copyrighted software
- Planting viruses in someone else's computer system

People often have differing views of these legal-versus-ethical situations. Maybe you would object to firing an individual in a certain case while someone else would feel that firing was the "right" thing to do. Perhaps your understanding of a "just" cause conflicts with another person's; therefore, each of you would act differently in the same situation. Often, arguments on both sides of ethical issues are defensible.

A good first step in any ethical analysis is to get a professional assessment of the law and its ramifications. If the law is clear and the resolution lies in quadrants I or IV, no further investigation is warranted. When the law does not provide an answer, as when the dilemma falls in categories II or III, it is important to see if other factors shed more light on the dilemma. The next sections present such factors.

Guidelines

A *guideline* is something that leads us in a particular direction. Violating a guideline does not necessarily have the legal implications of breaking a law nor is such action necessarily unethical. Two kinds of guidelines can be used for discovering if an ethical dilemma exists and for arriving at a general direction for ethical action. *Informal guidelines* are brief questions or tests that help us quickly evaluate an action. *Formal guidelines* are more explicit statements of expected behavior.

Informal Guidelines

Following are some informal guidelines that can help us discover if an ethical dilemma exists.

Is there something you or others would prefer to keep quiet?

"Shushers." Is there a person or group in the situation who says, "Don't tell anybody . . . ," or "I hope no one finds out . . . ", or "Be sure X doesn't get wind of this"? The people making these statements are shushers. They are common in many *un*ethical situations. These people recognize unethical action but mistakenly feel it is justified if kept secret.

The Mom Test. Would you tell your mother what you did? Would you like it if your mother did what you did? This test simply discovers whether you would be proud or ashamed of an action. The Mom Test uses a highly personal reaction as the first indicator of a problem. For example, suppose you write a "word shock" program that makes up phrases and sentences from a pool of words the dictionary defines as vulgar. Would you brag to your Mom about it or would you try to keep her from finding out?

The TV Test. How would you feel if you saw your situation described on TV or in the *New York Times*? Would the story make you look good or bad? How would the millions of viewers or readers react? In this test, pretend your ethical dilemma is being publicized far and wide. For example, suppose you and your best friend are competing computer graphics consultants but, to save money, you decide to purchase and share one copy of all software. How would an article describing your decision reflect on your business and you?

The Market Test. Unlike the other informal guidelines, the Market Test identifies situations with a positive ethical flavor. If a situation passes the Market Test, it is more likely to be ethical. Would you use your behavior as a marketing tool? In other words, would publicizing your action reap praise or criticism for your organization? For instance, suppose you are developing a database containing numerous data elements that some people consider private, and you are planning to make this database available to anyone for a small fee. Would advertising this feature in a prominent national magazine bring praise to the organization? If not, the development of the database would fail the Market Test.

Does your instinct tell you that something is wrong?

The Smell Test. Does the situation "smell"? Do you just feel in your bones that there's a problem, but you can't pin it down? If so, there is a problem, because the situation has failed the Smell Test. For example, suppose you develop a program that takes text and paraphrases it in any style you choose. On the surface this program seems relatively innocent, but something just doesn't feel right. When you think about it at length, you discover potential problems. What if someone takes Mark Twain's works and uses your program to rewrite them in the style of Hawthorne? Could the customer produce a "long-lost Hawthorne manuscript"? What else might happen?

Formal Guidelines

The questions that follow apply to formal guidelines, which you may find helpful in solving the ethical problems you face as an information professional or computer user. The responses to various questions may give contradictory advice. But by working through the questions, you can gain a clearer picture of the dilemma and, perhaps, the beginnings of an ethical solution.

1. Does the act violate corporate policy? Either explicitly or implicitly, corporations often tell their employees how to act. The policy may be a rule stating that no gifts are to be accepted from vendors, or it may just be a motto, such as "The customer is always right." Both of these policies are guides to individual action.

2. Does the act violate corporate or professional codes of conduct or ethics? Often, companies and professional organizations adopt such codes. Some are quite specific and can be helpful in directing the activities of the members. Even if you do not belong to a professional society or your organization does not have a computer ethics code, it may be worthwhile to adopt a code as your personal guide.

3. Does the act violate the Golden Rule? That is, are you treating others the way you would wish them to treat you? What if the roles were reversed, if you were in the other person's shoes? Would you be happy if the act were done to you? If you wouldn't want the roles reversed, then there is probably something wrong. For example, suppose your company develops a database management system that your client wants desperately—indeed, the client is even willing to pay a bonus for early release. You know there are bugs in the program as it is now, but you decide to sell it early anyway and use the bonus to debug the product more quickly. Then you can send your client a new version. Would you like to be the client? If not, the situation fails the Golden Rule.

Ethical Principles

So far, this chapter has presented practical approaches to discovering ethical dilemmas and setting a direction for ethical action. Sometimes, however, the practical approach is not enough to solve a problem. It may help us to discover the ethical dilemma and even convince us which action is wrong. But it may not go far enough in telling us why. This is where ethical principles help. They provide sound reasons for ethical behavior that not only solve the dilemma at hand, but also allow the lesson learned to be applied to other similar situations. Arguments are stripped of emotion, and commonly held principles or beliefs are substituted for intuition. The sections that follow will introduce you to several principles: rights and duties, consequentialism, and Kant's idea of the categorical imperative.

Rights and Duties*

The study of rights and duties is *deontology*. The term comes from the Greek word *deon*, which means duty. Having an understanding of rights and duties is helpful in analyzing ethical situations and making an ethical choice. The notion of responsibility is a part of this discussion.

Considering Rights. Rights are inherent universal privileges, that is, privileges that we consider our due by reason of law, tradition, or nature. The U.S. Constitution's Bill of Rights, for example, safeguards important political rights. The field of information technology frequently involves questions about three specific rights:

- *The right to know:* To what extent do we have a right to know, and have access to, the information that relates to us in a database? What rights do other people have to know and access the information that relates to them if it exists in our database?

- *The right to privacy:* To what extent do we have a right to control the use of information that relates to us? For example, should our personal medical information be accessible only to the people we authorize to use it? What privacy rights do others have in regard to the data we hold about them?

- *The right to property:* To what extent do we have a right to protect our computer resources from misuse and abuse? For example, what measures can we take to prevent viruses from being planted or our software from being copied?

Considering Duties. When we do something because it is a duty, we feel compelled by a moral obligation and the action cannot be avoided. According to the world's moralists, all human beings have certain duties in

*This discussion and the discussion of consequentialism are based on discussions at The Ethics Gadfly Workshop held at the Center for Business Ethics, Bentley College, Waltham, Massachusetts, during the summer of 1991. Dr. W. Michael Hoffman and Dr. M. Francis Reeves conducted the workshop under a grant from General Electric Corporation.

common. These duties are the basis for our definition of rights. A person who has rights has corresponding duties—duties that are expected of an individual in society. Furthermore, one person's rights may require duties by another.

The moral obligations in the list that follows are common to almost all cultures. They form the basis for most of the value-laden judgments that a human being makes.

Each person has the personal duty:

- *To foster trust:* Trust occurs when others have confidence that our work is competent, timely, and will not cause harm.

- *To act with integrity:* Acting with integrity allows others to depend on our honesty.

- *To be truthful:* Others should be able to expect us to be truthful and to act with fidelity.

- *To do justice:* Justice is served when our dealings with others are fair. Justice demands that those who perform services are rightfully paid and that wrongful acts are deservedly punished.

- *To practice beneficence and nonmaleficence:* Acts of beneficence help others improve their lot. Nonmaleficence prohibits causing harm to others.

- *To act with appropriate gratitude and make appropriate reparation:* Gratitude is being thankful for the kind acts of others; reparation is the act of providing fair recompense for wrongful acts done to others.

- *To work toward self-improvement:* When we improve our moral and mental faculties, such as by not committing a wrong a second time, we are acting according to the duty of self-improvement.

A concept closely related to duty is responsibility, which is a duty that is usually well defined and specific to a profession. Information professionals share the duties we all have as individuals, and in addition they have professional responsibilities that apply to them because of their specialized skills and knowledge.

When a person accepts employment in any position, he or she accepts moral responsibilities that define appropriate behavior in that job. These responsibilities are often referred to as *professional ethics*. Two factors apply to all professionals and influence their actions: professional relationships and professional efficacy, the latter meaning that professionals have the power to produce specific effects.

- *Professional relationships:* Professionals have relationships with employers, clients, co-workers, and others. These relationships are different from relationships with parents, spouse, and friends. For one thing, professional relationships may be specifically defined, even in a written contract. They are carried out within a framework of laws, customs, and policies. For example, an employee has a responsibility to perform a full day's work. The corresponding duty on the part of the employer is to reward that work equitably.

■ *Professional efficacy:* Professionals have some skill or knowledge through which they produce some product or service. Because they have the power, they also have the obligation to use it in a way that reduces harm or increases the public good. For example, a computer consultant proposes a new system with a one-year development period. The client claims to need the system in six months. The professional knows that a system delivered that soon will not do the job and may, in fact, cause serious harm to the client and those the client serves. Professional efficacy demands that the consultant explain the reality to the client and, if necessary, refuse the assignment.

Information professionals have the additional responsibilities of maintaining confidentiality and impartiality.

■ *Confidentiality* demands that a professional protect information from unauthorized access and use. Consider this situation: Thomas is a financial analyst who uses a computer terminal daily to access information about stocks and bonds. One day he discovers that his terminal can also access the medical database that contains information about his fellow employees. He has no need for this information in the daily performance of his job. His *duty* is to notify his superior that he has access to this database, because it is providing an avenue for violating the confidentiality that his fellow employees have a *right* to expect.

■ *Impartiality* demands that a professional be fair and impartial, treating all parties equally so that professional services can be provided without bias. For instance, impartiality demands that a software firm make new releases available to all customers, on the same basis.

The Relationship Between Rights and Duties. Any person who has a right also has a corresponding duty. For example, a computer manager has a right to choose between several competing software products. That same manager has a corresponding duty to choose the one that best serves the organization. You may visualize this relationship between rights and duties this way:

A's right ⟶ A's duty

Conversely, if you recognize that a person has a specific duty, this leads to that person having a corresponding right. For example, if a software manufacturer has a duty to provide an efficient and reliable product, it has a right to a fair return on its investment.

A's duty ⟶ A's right

Another way to consider rights and duties is to discover who else is involved. For example, if it is the software manufacturer's duty to provide an efficient and reliable product, it is the customer's right to expect the same. On the other hand, if the manufacturer has a right to a fair return, the customer has a corresponding duty to pay for the product and not use or make pirated copies. The combined interactions of rights and duties look like this:

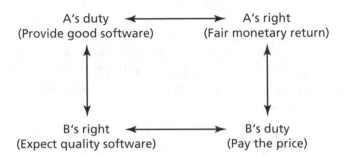

A's duty ⟷ A's right
(Provide good software) (Fair monetary return)

B's right ⟷ B's duty
(Expect quality software) (Pay the price)

Consequentialism

When we focus on the goals, ends, results, or consequences of an action, we are using the principle of *consequentialism*. Another word for consequentialism is *teleology*, which comes from the Greek word *telos*, or goal. We judge the rightness or wrongness of an action by the outcomes.

A common standard for deciding right from wrong involves the outcome of *harm minimization*. This means choosing the course of action that minimizes the amount of harm (actual or potential), thus leading to a less unsatisfactory solution to an ethical problem. A corollary to this approach is considering the greater good, which leads to a more satisfactory decision. As an individual, if you make these standards a part of your everyday toolkit, you may discover that they afford you an unexpected advantage. If you bear in mind harm minimization or the greater good, you are more likely to spot ethical problems as well as solve them.

The three major types of consequentialism are egoism, utilitarianism, and altruism.

Egoism is operating when you wish to maximize benefit to yourself, or minimize harm to yourself, with less consideration given to others. The principle of *utilitarianism* allows you to consider primarily the good (or harm) to others affected by your decision. Your reasoning is not self-centered but group-centered, seeking the maximum benefit for the group. The size of that group depends on the situation, but you are a part of it. *Altruism* is invoked when you sacrifice something to benefit others. You may suffer some harm, but the interests of others are advanced.

The lines between these are not always clear. Actions may not fall cleanly into a single category and may overlap categories to a greater or lesser degree. For example, when a business or individual donates to charity, that is a form of altruism. However, if the business or person benefits in some way from this action, either through favorable publicity or from services provided, some degree of egoism is present.

Deciding Ethical Questions Through Egoism.   Egoism relates to the concept of long-term rationality, which is also called enlightened self-interest or prudence. If an action won't help you in the long term, it may be foolish, or imprudent. We use this ethical principle as justification when we do something that furthers our own welfare. It is sometimes helpful to think of this as the "good for me" principle or the "ethics of arrogance," because we may subordinate higher-quality ethical outcomes to those that serve our own advantage. On the other hand, self-interest, in the form of a company seeking to increase its profits, is a valid justification for many business actions. This is an illustration of the kind of ambiguity that can result from ethical analysis—that is, egoism may be justified in certain circumstances and not in others. A decision maker who relies on a single principle without consideration of other principles may be led to inappropriate conclusions. Egoism needs to be guided and limited by other ethical principles.

If an individual feels threatened, either by having his or her actions detected or by the possibility of punishment for those actions, egoism has probably been misapplied. The individual's actions may have passed the "good for me" test but are ethically insupportable because of possible harm to others. For example, suppose you discover in an obscure journal a highly efficient algorithm for sorting records. You decide to incorporate it into your production software, and you take credit for it as your own idea. As a result, you feel threatened by the possible detection of your act and you fear punishment. In this case, you based your actions on self-interest only; the principle of egoism was not supported by any other principle. You did not consider the possible harm that your decision could cause to others. As you will see in the discussion of utilitarianism, it can be advantageous to consider others in your analysis.

To return to the example of the premature release of database management software on page 12: Suppose many customers have already paid deposits, and some have paid the full price; they are desperate for this program. However, it hasn't been tested thoroughly, and now Alice, the product manager, has to decide whether the program should be released. She decides that her reputation is at stake, so she releases the program to the customers. Did she consider all the consequences? Was she acting solely on the basis of her interests (the ethics of arrogance)? What are the consequences of her actions? What if all software developers always released their products on the advertised release date?

Deciding Ethical Questions Through Utilitarianism.   When our actions benefit others as well as ourselves, we are operating in the public interest. We measure the usefulness, or utility, of our actions not only for ourselves, but for everyone involved. This approach embodies the principle of utilitarianism, which helps a person judge, through a form of cost-benefit analysis, whether an action is ethical. Using this principle, an action is judged to be right if it maximizes benefits over costs for all involved, everyone counting equally.

For example, consider Alice, the product manager of the software company already mentioned. Suppose she notifies all potential customers that the software will be delayed during an intensive period of final testing. She has measured the importance of the reputation of her company against some possible lost sales and decided that the greater benefit lies in protecting the company's name. Also, by informing the customers of the delay, she is serving the public interest by allowing customers and others to make alternate arrangements.

Now consider a company that provides sufficient security to protect the sensitive data files of its clients. The company is acting in accord with utilitarianism, even though it increases costs and lowers profits to the firm's stockholders.

Deciding Ethical Questions Through Altruism. Altruism is invoked when a decision results in benefit for others, even at a cost to some. For example, a company may reduce the profit margin on its products and apply the difference to an environmental cause such as reforestation or wildlife conservation. We are altruistic when we give blood to the Red Cross or donate to a charity.

Altruism can be misapplied. Consider the university librarian who donates a CD-ROM containing nationwide names and phone numbers and makes it available on-line to anyone who accesses the library system. Some users who have unlisted phone numbers will be distressed to find that they are on the CD-ROM because the data came from sources other than the phone company. The librarian's well-meaing sacrifice of money and time will backfire.

Kant's Categorical Imperative

The 18th-century philosopher Immanuel Kant considered it absolutely necessary for a person to treat others equally and with respect. He suggested two principles for examining whether a person has the right to act a certain way in a given situation. He referred to these principles as *consistency* and *respect*. The principles of consistency and respect are aspects of what Kant called the categorical imperative.

Applying the Principle of Consistency. The principle of consistency asks us all to be fair in our actions. This demands of us more than simply treating everyone equally, though this is a part of the requirement. It also implies a refusal to do something if we think some harm might result if everyone were to do it. When you test an action to see if it meets the principle of consistency, you ask yourself, "Would everyone benefit (or would no one be harmed) if everyone were to take the action being considered?" If not, do not take it. For example, if everyone lied, how would we ever know the truth? Or, if everyone copied software rather than buying it, how could we expect anyone to offer software for sale?

Applying the Principle of Respect. This principle suggests that we treat people with dignity. In other words, people are ends in themselves, not means. If we use people as slaves, we deny their humanness and do not show them respect. Thus, slavery violates the categorical imperative. In the computer field, performing electronic surveillance on employees without their knowledge might be considered an act of disrespect and a violation of the categorical imperative.

Considering Stakeholders

A *stakeholder* is any person or organization with a stake in the decision. In performing any ethical analysis, more than one stakeholder (person or organization) is involved. These stakeholders have different and often competing concerns and interests. When we review various tests and apply ethical principles, the focus of our thinking is on the effect our actions will have on the stakeholders. We may not be able to satisfy all stakeholders equally or even ensure that all receive a positive outcome. But a thoughtful ethical analysis should result in a defensible ethical decision, and one that on balance does the "best" for all concerned. This will be illustrated in Chapter 3.

SUMMARY

Everyone has the obligation to understand ethics. Making ethical choices is part of everyday life, especially for those who use and create information technology. Ethical situations involving computers take many forms. Often, however, the participants in the situations do not realize ethics is involved.

In making ethical choices, following a logical approach and applying commonly held principles usually leads to higher-quality decisions than relying on intuition or personal preference alone. The logical approach helps to assure a thorough analysis. The resulting principled decisions are based on specific reasons and are more easily defended. Furthermore, once made, their lesson is easily transferred to other similar issues. Intuition, on the other hand, leads to generalities that often lack clear justification. Thus the key to dealing with ethical dilemmas is to follow a structured approach to discovering them and a rational process for resolving them. In Chapter 2, we offer a fuller explanation of the ethical challenges computers pose.

ANNOTATED REFERENCES

Bologna, J. A framework for the ethical analysis of information technologies, *Computers & Security*, October 1991, 303–307.

> Contains some worthwhile insights into ethical analysis and decision making.

Hoffman, W. M., and R. E. Frederick, Eds. *Business Ethics: Readings and Cases in Corporate Morality,* 3d ed., New York: McGraw-Hill, 1995, 577–584.

An extensive readings book on business ethics, with a number of classic articles on ethical theory and business decision making.

Johnson, D. G. *Computer Ethics*, 2d ed., Englewood Cliffs, NJ: Prentice-Hall, 1994.

A thorough explanation of computer ethics and the application of ethical principles to computer situations. Various scenarios are explored from differing ethical perspectives. A good supplement to Chapter 1.

Smith, H. J., and E. A. Kallman. Toward a global IT ethics, *Beyond Computing*, September 1994, 24–25.

A brief exposition of some of the special ethical circumstances faced in global information technology management.

Wagner, J. L. Using a taxonomy of ethical situations in MIS, 1991 *Journal/ Proceedings Information Systems and Quantitative Management*, Midwest Business Administration Association, 1991, 112–118.

A clear exposition on the relationship between law and ethics.

Weiss, J. *Business Ethics: A Managerial, Stakeholder Approach,* Belmont, CA: Wadsworth, 1994.

An explanation of the stakeholder approach to ethical decision making as well as coverage of other approaches to solving general business ethical dilemmas.

Chapter

2

Ethics and Information Technology

NEW TECHNOLOGY, NEW PROBLEMS

Computers have changed forever the way we conduct business and live our lives. Each new year of the Information Age means more and faster processing by smaller and more powerful computers. In their special way, computers have compressed time and space. Today, computers perform processes and provide services that were formerly impossible. We can make airline reservations instantly, get cash from a teller machine, and send electronic mail around the world. Computer capabilities are still expanding and are not expected to level off in the foreseeable future.

The amazing abilities of computers present new ethical challenges. Chapter 1 mentioned a few characteristics that typify "computer" ethics. Chapter 2 will expand this discussion by showing how the unique natures of computers and humans contribute to ethical dilemmas. The chapter will then list ethical issues that pertain to specific aspects of information technology. Some of these issues, such as computer crime, are obvious. Others, such as an employer's obligation to provide an ergonomically sound computing environment, are less so. The purpose of this chapter is to sensitize you to all the aspects of information technology that involve ethics. If at some future time you think to yourself, "There is an ethical dilemma here, and I need to analyze it before I go on," then the chapter will have achieved its goal.

WHY IS ETHICAL COMPUTER USE A SPECIAL CHALLENGE?

Managing computers ethically—that is, acting ethically and assisting others to do likewise—is no easy task for either an individual or an organization. Donn Parker, Susan Swope, and Bruce Baker (all of SRI International), claim that "the application of ethics in information science, technology, and business is more difficult than in other disciplines" (Parker, Swope, and Baker, 1990). In explaining why, the three authors cite several unique aspects of computers and computer use.

Difficulties Posed by Computers

Parker, Swope, and Baker offer these reasons why ethical problems involving computers pose a special challenge.

- Using computers and data communications alters the relationships among people. Personal contact is reduced, and the speed of communication often does not give the participant time to reflect on the possibility or implications of unethical use.

- When information is in electronic form, it is far more "fragile" than when it is on paper. It is more easily changed, and more vulnerable to unauthorized access. A related problem is that it can be reproduced again and again with no degradation of quality, unlike data recorded on paper. The questions of property rights, plagiarism, piracy, and privacy become active issues.

- Efforts to protect information integrity, confidentiality, and availability often conflict with the desire for the benefits of information sharing.

- The lack of widespread means of authorization and authentication exposes information technology to unethical practice.

The computer's unique nature is only part of the reason why ethical computer use is so hard to enforce. Humans also contribute to ethical dilemmas, as the following section will show.

Difficulties Posed by the Pace of Technological Change

Scientists and graphic artists are familiar with the *order-of-magnitude effect*. This says that, for each tenfold increase (that is, an increase of one order of magnitude) in speed, our perception of what is going on changes dramatically. When a motion picture photographer takes a time-lapse shot, say of a flower blooming, and then plays it for us at normal film speed, our perception of the blooming flower is entirely different from what actually took place in real time. Because of the order-of-magnitude effect, we see the flower blooming as if it were not a flower at all but perhaps a miniature explosion.

Computer hardware technology increases in all measures of power exponentially; disk capacity and processor speed, for example, roughly double every two to three years. This simple fact poses problems because societal changes occur much more slowly. This cultural lag, well explained in Alvin Toffler's book *Future Shock,* presents us with multiple dilemmas when we consider the ethics of computer use.

In 1988, personal computer owners were thankful to have a 10-megabyte disk drive for $1,000. For this amount today, we can buy a drive with many times that capacity that is faster and more reliable than earlier models. Predictions arc for even more speed and capacity in the near future. What are the implications of access to that much data? How can the data be managed, protected, kept accurate? Will new capabilities in video and voice processing create as yet unanticipated ethical problems?

As a consequence of information technology's rapid growth, we are forced to adapt to its newest features on a continuing basis. There is pressure to keep up with the "cutting edge" so that our organizations are competitive. To use the deluge of new software and hardware takes extensive training. We can barely manage to learn the new technologies before they change and, as a result, we often pay scant attention to the consequences of their use.

It is because computers operate at a speed that is several orders of magnitude faster than human activity that we use computers to manage many of our important affairs. Our daily dealings with computers tend to mask their rapidly increasing power. Much as human aging goes unnoticed from day to day, the power increases have happened without our being aware of them. Eventually, however, we must recognize that these extraordinary advances in computer power are not necessarily neutral in their impact and, therefore, we must adapt our ethical stance accordingly. One way to understand the computer's increasing speed and capacity is through a related phenomenon, which we call the effort effect.

The Effort Effect

The principle of unreasonable effort, or the *effort effect,* maintains that if a task is not worth the effort, people will tend not to undertake it. Consider an example that relates to information technology. Processed with a manual system or even an early computer, a data file of personnel records could be considered relatively secure for several reasons: getting the data into some meaningful form would take a long time; the data access might require a number of people; and by the time the data was organized, it might well have lost its value. In other words, even though access was not denied, privacy was ensured because wrongdoing required too much effort.

If new technology reduces the amount of effort, however, people are likely to undertake new projects that use the technology. Newspaper reporters on one local paper provided an example of this.* The reporters

*Dean, Cory. Computer use for news raises legal questions, *New York Times*, Sept. 29, 1986, A12.

obtained computerized information on more than 30,000 state-subsidized mortgages. Through elementary computer processing, they uncovered a scandal in the state mortgage agency. This could never have been detected using only manual methods. The information had always been available, but it was "secure" because of the difficulty in obtaining it.

Ten years ago, a database containing the names, addresses, and buying habits of 120 million people (more than the populations of England and France combined) would have been too expensive and too large to create. Access to any worthwhile information would have been too slow. Today, such a database can fit on several CD-ROMs, its data can be accessed with a personal computer, and its cost is so low that a major software manufacturer considered such a database a real opportunity. Is it really inconceivable, then, that in 10 years we could have a "world database" of personal information about everyone? Who would have access to this world database? Everyone, or just a few? What would it be used for? How would it be controlled?

In the early 1980s, timesharing mainframe computers were still fairly new. Today, an individual with a personal computer can access international networks, often for an access fee of just a few dollars. How can we get ready for the Information Superhighway of the 21st century, which will connect us all electronically? What will be its effect on our privacy? And what ethical dilemmas will accompany it?

With the effort effect in mind, we will now look more closely at specific unethical activity.

WHAT IS UNETHICAL COMPUTER USE?

Unethical computer use takes many forms, is performed by people inside and outside organizations, and occurs with computers of all sizes and capabilities, both standalone and networked. Networked computers are much less secure because of their "outside" connection; therefore, they are more vulnerable to unethical activity. But in spite of the publicity that hackers have received, most unethical computer activity is performed by people inside a firm, quite often by disgruntled employees. Furthermore, harm occurs and ethical problems arise not only in the use of the computer, but in all the tasks performed by information systems professionals and those who work with them.

The remainder of this chapter will present, by category, specific ethical issues relating to information technology.

Social and Economic Issues

Job displacement caused by new information technology is an important ethical issue. Many who lose their jobs to "information machines" can be retrained, and the Information Age has spawned new professions, such as those of the computer programmer and systems analyst. But computers do cause displacement, and the ethical dilemma involves minimizing the hardship to those affected.

Another social aspect of computerization concerns the work-related demands placed on computer professionals. Computer work is pressure-filled; it always seems to be behind schedule. This results in long hours, often stretched over weekends and holidays. Family problems and divorce rates are high in the profession. This raises the ethical question, is management being fair?

The third social issue involves power and access to it. We have already shown that computers are part of our everyday existence. We need them to live the kind of lives we want to lead. But what of those who do not have access to computers? What about children in an inner-city school system without computer courses? If the students are not computer literate, will they be able to compete on an equal footing with those who are? Do they have a right to equal computer access? Do they have less power than those who have access? This issue has been raised in regard to who will be able to travel the Information Superhighway. Many people advocate that "on-ramps" be provided to all citizens, especially if the highway is government funded.

Issues of Individual Practice

An individual who uses a computer, whether on the job or for personal use, has the responsibility to use it ethically. On an everyday level, this means that each of us must use ethical practices. We must protect passwords and change them frequently. We must not share passwords or choose ones that are so obvious that anyone could guess them. We must protect the computer resource by saving files periodically; backing up files regularly; and locking up removable disks, perhaps off-site. When actually using the computer, we should take care not to leave confidential information unattended on the screen. Similarly, we should protect hardcopy, especially if it is sent to a shared printer.

Software Development Issues

This book has already presented a number of examples involving an important ethical issue that relates to the development process: the issue of an incomplete or unreliable program that fails to do what is expected. Suppose a development team rushes a program to meet a deadline—perhaps to coincide with the introduction of a new product or to avoid the wrath of management. Or maybe the team performs insufficient systems analysis resulting in the program being based on incomplete specifications.

Issues of systems development involve computer professionals who, because of their specialized knowledge, bear certain responsibilities. These are the professional duties discussed in Chapter 1. When they say a program is fully tested, they are believed because they are professionals. When they mislead their clients, they violate professional ethics and damage the profession and themselves. A shoddy program can damage the client as well.

Another ethical issue that relates to the development process is software piracy, the unauthorized copying of software. It is estimated that as much as 50 percent of all programs used on personal computers are pirated copies. In some countries, the estimate is as high as 99 percent. The most common excuse for pirating software is that the individual or organization cannot afford to buy it, and without it, the person or firm would be at a disadvantage.

Issues Involving Managers and Subordinates

Organizations consist of multiple levels of authority and responsibility. These differing levels of personal power can lead to ethical dilemmas. Three examples follow.

- Because she feels she should have been promoted instead of someone else, a programmer plants a "bomb" program to destroy a program she knows is important to the company.

- A financial analyst terminated due to downsizing puts erroneous data into the organization's computer files prior to leaving.

- A manager demands that a programmer write an accounting routine that the programmer feels does not conform to Generally Accepted Accounting Principles.

Computer Processing Issues

Computer processing issues include two types of problems: unreliability and late output.

Problems of Unreliability

Ethical issues arising from the operation of computers to a great extent involve hardware and software unreliability and the failure to anticipate it. These dilemmas occur, in part, because of the increasing degree of application complexity, and the growing dependence of organizations and individuals on computers. As applications and the computers they run on become more complex, they are harder to test, fix, and operate without interruption or error. As people and organizations become more dependent on computers, they are more inconvenienced by any unreliability in the system. In fact, actual harm may result, as in the case of an airliner crash caused by the failure of an air-controller's computer. Or it may be as simple as a faulty ATM that forces a person in need of cash to seek another machine. In both cases, a promised service is not delivered, and harm or inconvenience results. Did the developers have contingency plans? Did they work? If not, why not?

Problems of Late Output

As an example of late output, consider the case of a late-clearing check that prevents an anticipated purchase or embarrasses the innocent depositor. Who is responsible when this happens? What should or can be done about it?

Issues Relating to the Workplace

The two primary issues in this category are ergonomics and employee monitoring.

Ergonomics

Ergonomics is concerned with the physical work environment. The question is, how far should an organization go to be "ergonomically sound"? For example, what is required to provide data entry clerks with a healthful work area? How can a firm create an environment that results in minimal eyestrain, guards against back problems, prevents repetitive-motion syndrome, and protects against exposure to possibly harmful CRT (cathode-ray tube) emissions?

Monitoring

Monitoring in this context means tracking and measuring employee activity. Activities tracked might include number of keystrokes, error rate, and number of transactions processed. What are the ethics of using technology to keep track of employee performance? Is it ethical to monitor phone calls by computer to determine a caller's number, when he or she called, and how long the call lasted? Should a supervisor listen in on a call? Such monitoring systems are not necessarily illegal. Elements of the ethical issue include the following:

- Does the employee or caller know about the monitoring?
- Does he or she understand how the information is to be used?
- Does he or she agree to its use?

Issues of Data Collection, Storage, and Access

These issues relate to the need to protect data confidentiality, privacy, and accuracy. How much data do you collect? Only what you need, or all you can get? Some argue that you ought to collect it now in case you need it in the future. Is this a justifiable position? For instance, should a human resources department collect and store police-record data about employees when there is no current need for that data? Is the data obtained with or without the permission or knowledge of the subject? Under what circumstances should you seek permission from or inform those whose records are on file?

How accurate is the data we obtain? For that matter, how accurate does data need to be? For example, the quality of some marketing decisions might not be diminished by using slightly inaccurate sales data. On the other hand, there would be great potential for harm if a medical record was inaccurate.

How much effort should be made to correct errors? Is it feasible or necessary for the data file to be 100 percent accurate? Does the subject of the data have the opportunity to examine the file to detect and correct errors?

Who has access to the data? Who knows what persons have exercised access privileges? Who knows what persons have tried to exercise access privileges but failed because they were unauthorized? Should we keep logs of all successful and unsuccessful accesses? What effort has been made to protect the data from theft? How long do we keep data?

How do we prevent the unintended use of data? Should data be collected for one purpose and then arbitrarily used for something else? For example, should a credit card company, without the cardholder's knowledge, use information about credit card purchases to create a consumer profile for marketing purposes? The key aspect of this issue is permission. The cardholders may have agreed to have information about their purchases recorded, but they may not have given permission to be profiled and for that profile to be distributed to others. The practice of computer matching comes under this category—for example, when the Internal Revenue Service compares its tapes with other agencies' tapes to catch parents who fail to pay child support.

Who owns the data? Answering this will often resolve some of the earlier questions. Ownership implies certain rights and responsibilities. Usually the owner is responsible for error detection and correction. But ownership needs to be defined and agreed upon by all parties; this is not an easy task.

Issues Involving Electronic Mail and the Internet

These issues are becoming more important because of the increasing popularity of e-mail. The question is not whether the owner of the e-mail system has the right to monitor its contents. This right of oversight for an organization's internal systems has been fairly well established. The question is, to what extent should an owner exercise this right and under what circumstances? Some of the issues raised in our discussion of monitoring surface here as well. The concepts of "full disclosure" and "informed consent" apply here. E-mail systems may be served best by owners who fully disclose their privacy policies and practices. Such openness leads to informed users.

The Internet and the anticipated Information Superhighway usher in a new set of ethical issues. The vast amount of information accessible raises the intellectual property rights questions of data ownership, copyright enforcement, and plagiarism. On another level, the nature and variety of the many thousands of discussion groups raise the issues of free speech and censorship and whether material offensive to some may be kept off the network.

Resource Exploitation Issues

This category includes wasting resources, interrupting services, and taking advantage of vulnerable systems. Some examples of resource exploitation follow.

- *Planting viruses:* Viruses are programs that reproduce themselves and destroy or alter other programs or data.

- *Hacking:* Hackers are people who break into computers to plant viruses, read files, steal data, or alter programs. Recently, some reformed hackers have offered their expertise to help firms protect against other hackers. This presents a special ethical dilemma: Should unethical, and in most cases illegal, practice be rewarded in this way?

- *Planting logic bombs:* Logic bombs are programs or pieces of programs that maliciously destroy data, other programs, or hardware. These bombs are often planted by disgruntled employees or political, social, or religious zealots who attempt to use the technology to achieve their own end.

- *Using another's computer for personal gain:* Some of the computer use in this category is "casual" and likened to taking pens and pads home from the office. But some employees have been discovered running an outside personal business using their employer's computer. In addition, e-mail provides a unique set of opportunities for the abuse of another's resource. For instance, it is quite easy to fill an e-mail network with extraneous messages. Simply sending personal messages on your employer's e-mail system without permission may be unethical. Some firms have had to restrict Internet use because of the time employees waste on discussion groups and other services that are not job related.

Vendor-Client Issues

This category encompasses all situations in which one party, the vendor, is supplying hardware, software, or a service to another party, the client. Vendor-client issues generally involve payment for the services rendered. The vendor provides a service for a fee, and the client pays the fee and receives that service. The contract that binds the two parties implies or explicitly states the obligations of each party. Such contracts are becoming larger and more complex as the practice of "outsourcing" becomes prevalent. When a company outsources, it contracts with an outside agency to serve the company's computing needs. The agency could provide anything from development of a computer system to day-to-day computer operations.

Ethical issues in this category are usually related to non-performance according to the terms of the contract and disagreements over implied warranties. Suppose a vendor fails to deliver software by the promised date. Or suppose the software is delivered but it lacks the promised functionality. In one famous incident* a firm decided that the programs written by a software vendor did not meet its specifications. When the firm could get no satisfaction from the vendor, it withheld further payment, which is a common business practice. But the software vendor had embedded a routine in several programs that would prevent them from being used if the firm stopped paying. The vendor activated the routine, the firm could no longer use the programs, and the firm's operations were severely affected. The vendor maintained that the product had been "repossessed" because of non-payment.

Some other common examples of ethical dilemmas in client-vendor relations follow.

- A user continually changes system specifications, resulting in delays and added expense to the developer. This situation can even occur between a user and a systems analyst who both work for the same firm. Though an outside vendor is not involved, the client-vendor relationship and the responsibility to act ethically still exist.

- A consultant sells a program to a second client after being paid to develop that software exclusively for the first client.

- A vendor provides hardware maintenance according to a written contract that calls for hardware to be repaired in a "timely manner." The client does not believe that repairs have been timely.

Issues of Computer Crime

This area involves using the computer as a tool to perform illegal acts such as fraud, embezzlement, and the like. Experts believe the number of crimes committed far exceeds the number reported. Firms seem reluctant to report computer crimes. Managers are embarrassed that they let the crime happen, and they know that prosecuting perpetrators is difficult. However, the failure to prosecute does not in any way diminish the importance of computer crime or the size of the risk to individuals and firms resulting from the crimes. The incidence of computer crime is rising, as is the magnitude of the harm it generates.

One computer crime that is getting increasing attention is the use of imaging and desktop publishing technology to create, copy, or alter official documents and graphic images. This is an example of how technological change spawns ever-changing threats.

---

*Cusack, Sally. Revlon riles software vendor, *Computerworld*, Oct. 29, 1990, 6.

SUMMARY

Because computers permeate our work and personal lives, all of us have an obligation to see that they are used responsibly. The factors that characterize ethical dilemmas in a computer environment include the speed of a computer, vulnerability of computer data to unauthorized change, and the fact that protecting information often decreases its accessibility. Because of the effort effect, harmless situations may turn into harmful ones without our realizing it. The elimination of the effort required to access and organize large quantities of data poses its own threat.

The social implications of information technology include such issues as job displacement, power, and access. As individuals, we have the responsibility to protect resources and confidentiality by employing sound computer practices. Other ethical issues relate to systems development; manager-subordinate relations; computer processing; workplace design and practices; data collection, storage, and access; e-mail and the Internet; misuse of another's resources; vendor-client relations; and crime.

ANNOTATED REFERENCES

Harrington, A. Computer crime and abuse by IS employees, *Journal of Systems Management*, March/April 1995, 6–11.

An analysis of the problems facing IS management caused by members of their own organization.

Kallman, E. A., and S. Sherizen. Private matters, *Computerworld*, (In Depth), November 23, 1992, 85–87.

An explanation of e-mail privacy issues and suggestions for organizational management.

Mason, R., F. Mason, and M. Culnan. *Information and Responsibility: The Ethical Challenge*, Thousand Oaks, CA: Sage Publications, 1995.

A thoughtful analysis of the relationship between ethics and information management. Explains the importance of information, the essence of ethical thinking, and management responsibility for both.

Ofeldt, R., and E. A. Kallman. Electronic monitoring of employees: issues and guidelines, *Journal of Systems Management*, June 1993, 17–21.

An overview of the issues surrounding employee monitoring. Offers some suggestions for creating a successful monitoring program to benefit both the organization and the employee.

Parker, D., S. Swope, and B. Baker. *Ethical Conflicts in Information and Computer Science, Technology, and Business*, Wellesley, MA: QED Information Sciences, 1990.

Describes a research project in which a panel of experts voted on how to respond to a number of ethical scenarios. Some useful insights into some computer ethical problems and their possible resolution.

Smith, H. J., and E. A. Kallman. Defining ethical feasibility, *Beyond Computing,* March/April 1995, 12–13.

Smith, H. J., and E. A. Kallman. Implementing a feasibility study, *Beyond Computing,* May 1995, 12–13.

Two related articles suggesting a process for assessing the ethicality of a computer application before it is approved for development.

Smith, H. J. *Managing Privacy: Information Technology and Corporate America,* Chapel Hill: University of North Carolina Press, 1994.

A practical look at information privacy as a serious management issue. Numerous real-world examples set out the details of the problem. Author provides well-drawn action steps applicable to any organization.

Toffler, A. *Future Shock,* New York: Bantam Books, 1971.

A brilliant insight into the impacts of change, which continues to have value to this day.

3

Solving Ethical Dilemmas
A Sample Case Exercise

A FOUR-STEP ANALYSIS PROCESS

In Chapter 1, you learned how to make defensible ethical decisions. The term *defensible* is important in this context. Although the emotions play an important role in the decision-making process, you have learned that defensible decisions are made by considering objective principles and weighing their effects on the issue. This process of logical analysis does more than help resolve a current dilemma; the analysis can help prevent or solve similar problems in the future.

In this chapter, you will employ the techniques you learned in Chapter 1 and expand on them. You will learn to recognize the relevant facts before you make an ethical decision, and you will see how to implement a decision and apply the fruits of your analysis to prevent the problem from recurring. The means to these skills is a four-step process presented in this chapter along with a case study. Step III of the process contains the decision-making approaches you learned in Chapter 1; other parts of the process will be new to you.

This chapter will apply the four-step process to the case study and provide extensive commentary. As you work through the steps, you may be surprised at the many levels of an ethical problem. As soon as one layer is "peeled" away, another appears. As ethical problem solvers, we must be sure we have exposed all the layers before implementing a decision; terminating analysis too soon may lead to a poor conclusion. The way to ensure consideration of all aspects is to complete the entire four-step process conscientiously.

Figure 3-1
A Four-Step Process
for Ethical Analysis and Decision Making

Step I. Understanding the situation
   A. List and number the relevant facts.
   B. Which of these raises an ethical issue? Why? What is the potential or resulting harm?
   C. List the stakeholders involved.

Step II. Isolating the major ethical dilemma
   What is the ethical dilemma to be resolved NOW? State it using the form: Should **someone** do or not do **something**? Note: Just state the dilemma here; leave any reasoning for Step III.

Step III. Analyzing the ethicality of both alternatives in Step II
Consequentialism
   A. If action in Step II is done, who, if anyone, will be harmed?
   B. If action in Step II is not done, who, if anyone, will be harmed?
   C. Which alternative results in the least harm, A or B?
   D. If action in Step II is done, who, if anyone, will benefit?
   E. If action in Step II is not done, who, if anyone, will benefit?
   F. Which alternative results in the maximum benefit, D or E?

Rights and Duties
   G. What **rights** have been or may be abridged? What **duties** have been or may be neglected? Identify the stakeholder and the right or duty. When listing a right, show its corresponding duty and vice versa.

Kant's Categorical Imperative
   H. If action in Step II is done, who, if anyone, will be treated with *dis*respect?
   I. If action in Step II is not done, who, if anyone, will be treated with *dis*respect?
   J. Which alternative is preferable, H or I?
   K. If action in Step II is done, who, if anyone, will be treated *un*like others?
   L. If action in Step II is not done, who, if anyone, will be treated *un*like others?
   M. Which alternative is preferable, K or L?
   N. Are there benefits if everyone did action in Step II?
   O. Are there benefits if nobody did action in Step II?
   P. Which alternative is preferable, N or O?

Step IV. Making a decision and planning the implementation
   A. Make a defensible ethical decision.
       Based on the analysis in Step III, respond to the question in Step II. Indicate the letters of the categories that best support your response. Add any arguments justifying your choice of these ethical principles to support your decision. Where there are conflicting rights and duties, choose and defend those that take precedence. (Note: Just make and justify your choice here; leave any action steps for parts B and D below.)
   B. List the specific steps needed to implement your defensible ethical decision.
   C. Show how the major stakeholders are affected by these actions.
   D. What other longer-term changes (political, legal, technical, societal, organizational) would help prevent such problems in the future?
   E. What should have been done or not done in the first place (at the pivot point) to avoid this dilemma?

To begin your study of the four-step analysis process, read the steps in Figure 3-1 in their entirety. For the sample case, we will respond to the process as though we were completing a worksheet like those found in Appendix B.

Examine the worksheet now and notice that the worksheet sections correspond to the entries in the figure. Perform the legal assessment and apply the guidelines in Figure 1-1 (page 9) to discover that something in the situation requires a closer look. Then carry out each step in Figure 3-1 to resolve the ethical dilemma.

SAMPLE CASE:
Too Much of a Good Thing? Workplace Monitoring Creates Privacy Dilemmas

Clare Valerian is a systems analyst at Califon, Inc., a large distributor of electronic equipment. Her primary responsibility is to make certain that the 127 end-users in Califon's U.S. headquarters can access data, post to accounts, send and receive e-mail, and accomplish all the other duties they need to perform on the corporation's local area network. She describes herself as a facilitator and troubleshooter. She must respond quickly to the users' complaints and needs, and even provide training for novice users. It's a demanding and time-consuming job, and until two weeks ago, Clare was spending up to 12 hours a day one-on-one with her users. She spent much of her time traveling to various sites in the different corporate buildings. The telephone was not much help, because Clare had to see for herself exactly what the users saw on their screens.

Recently, however, a utility program called LANSCAPE has changed her workday completely. The utility program and the telephone at her desk allow her to solve user problems without ever having to go directly to the users' workstations and terminals. The program allows Clare to view and actually take over the activities of network users. Typically, her first task upon arriving at her desk is to check her e-mail messages for trouble spots, print the messages, bring up LANSCAPE, and call each user one at a time.

"John, this is Clare in Systems. You left me a message about a problem with the inventory reorder module. I've got your screen up on my terminal now. Can you get out of the word processor and transfer to the inventory system? . . . Good. I see the main menu . . . Now, the reorder module. Go ahead and repeat the steps that got you into trouble yesterday. . . . OK, fine . . . oops, I see what you did. The system asks for ENTER and you hit RETURN. What kind of keyboard to you have? . . . That's what I thought. For now, remember to hit ENTER. I'll get the maintenance programmer to change the module to accept RETURN too. Sorry about that. . . . Thanks. Good-bye."

Then Clare goes on to the next call. "Bill, this is Clare in Systems. Your word processor bombed? Why don't you call it up and repeat the . . . oh, I see the problem. You're working with the buggy version, 2.3. I'll delete it from the system. You'll have to remember to use V2.4 from now on. . . . No problem. Good-bye."

Clare is delighted with the LANSCAPE utility. She roves electronically from one troubled user to another, seeing on her screen exactly what the user sees. The amount of time it takes to solve the problems is about the same, but because she can solve them from her desk, she has eliminated the frustrating delays of travel time. In addition, she is at her desk when the users call, and they are pleased with the fast response time.

Clare even has time to scan users' activities without their making a request. Her troubleshooting has become more proactive than reactive. She can scan a number of users without their knowledge, and when she finds one in trouble, she can interrupt and help.

"Harry, this is Clare in Systems. I'm looking at your screen now. . . . I know you didn't call, but I thought I'd beat you to the punch. You can speed up that multiple posting to a single customer by using the TAB key instead of updating the record for each entry. . . . Yes, like that. . . . Glad to be of service."

Last week Clare and her boss, the Director of User Support, met with the Vice President of Information Systems, Art Betony, to evaluate LANSCAPE. Clare said, "Without this program, I'd have to control the activities of every user in every system test and move from one building to the other. With LANSCAPE, I can watch over their shoulders without being there. LANSCAPE is inexpensive and easy to use. I fully endorse its continued use and recommend we obtain additional copies and make it available to all support personnel." The three went on to discuss the increase in user satisfaction and productivity that had resulted from the use of LANSCAPE.

Yesterday Art was having his usual Tuesday lunch with his boss, Executive Vice President Alberta Wilson. Art couldn't stop praising LANSCAPE.

Alberta seemed especially interested. "You mean you can tell me at any time what people are doing?"

"Not quite," Art answered. "We can only see the screens of the users who are logged in. But of course that's exactly what my people need for their purposes."

"But the people you observe this way . . . do they know their screens are being observed?"

"No, not unless we tell them. The LANSCAPE program doesn't change anything on their screens. Of course, that's a necessary feature of the system because my people have to see exactly what the users see."

"Could you install LANSCAPE on my terminal, in my office?"

"Of course. But what value would that be?"

Alberta leaned forward and whispered, "I shouldn't reveal this outside the Human Resources department, but I think I want to enlist your support. Here at headquarters, we may have one or more persons dealing in drugs. We have suspects but no proof. Somehow these people are taking orders and making deliveries right on the premises. And during company time. I suspect they're using the phone and maybe even the computer to make their deals. We tried various surveillance methods with no success. What I want to do is use LANSCAPE to randomly check on what the suspects are doing. Then, if we catch them red-handed, we'll have our evidence and we can prosecute."

Art frowned and said, "Gee, I don't know if I should give you that software, Alberta. Let me think about it and get back to you."

DISCOVERING AN ETHICAL DILEMMA

The following narrative illustrates the kind of reasoning and activity that could take place after Art's lunch with Alberta.

When Art leaves Alberta, he is bothered by a vague notion that Alberta's request poses some questions that must be resolved before he responds to her. He needs to discover whether there is an ethical dilemma that needs a closer look. The first thing he does is reflect on the current laws that may govern the situation. The illegality of the drug dealing is not in question. The main legal issue is whether monitoring in this situation is permitted. Though he is not a lawyer, Art does know something about laws in his professional area of information systems. Generally, under current law, it is not illegal to monitor employee activity. Recently proposed laws in some states would require official notification of employees. Employers must tell them (1) they are being monitored, (2) what information is being collected, and (3) what it is to be used for. Art concludes that using LANSCAPE internally, on company-owned systems, even without the knowledge of the employees, is legal. To remove any doubts about that conclusion, and to confirm his own position, he calls the company lawyer, who confirms that such monitoring activity is legal.

Even though the activity is legal, Art still feels there is an ethical dilemma. At this point he looks to guidelines for assistance. First he asks, "Is there something he or others would prefer to keep quiet?" On one hand, Alberta wants to keep her surveillance quiet. Clare, however, lets people know she is watching, although often only after the fact. Both approaches raise an ethical question.

Art then tries the Mom Test, but it is inconclusive. Clare's mom would probably be proud of the way Clare is being so helpful and productive, and she would certainly approve of catching the drug dealers. But Clare might not want to tell her how she invaded some innocent people's privacy. Even on nationwide TV (the TV Test), or through an ad in the *New York Times* (the Market Test), the monitoring could be portrayed as positive and praiseworthy. Applying the Smell Test, however, Art feels in his bones that there is a problem with Alberta's request.

You might conclude that the firm would not want to go on TV or take out the ad, because it would not want to admit that it suspected drug dealing on the premises. That, however, is not the point of these tests. The aim of the tests is to discover our level of "comfort" with our actions in response to an ethical dilemma. Art's problem is that he does not feel justified in performing the surveillance.

Since the tests so far do not give Art a clear direction, he then moves on to more formal guidelines. First, is the act consistent with corporate policy? Art Betony must find out if there is a policy on monitoring. Based on Alberta's admission of prior surveillance attempts, the form of which she doesn't explain, there may be a policy allowing monitoring. But the likelihood is that there is no policy at all. It is not unusual for even large organizations to have few explicit policies, especially concerning computer use. And often, even when there are policies, they are not well publicized or enforced. In this case, Art finds out that none exist. He also discovers that there is no corporate code of conduct or code for ethical computer use.

As for professional codes, since Art is a member of the Association for Computing Machinery (ACM), he decides to examine the ACM Code of Ethics and Professional Conduct (see Appendix A). Some imperatives that might apply are:

1.   General Moral Imperatives

As an ACM member I will . . .

1.1 Contribute to society and human well-being

Apprehending the drug dealers will certainly contribute to society. This imperative supports giving LANSCAPE to the executive V.P.

1.2 Avoid harm to others

Computer users who are not involved with drugs may be harmed if they are monitored. Their privacy might be violated. Personal messages, if they are permitted, may be revealed. Also, their actions may be subject to misinterpretation, as explained later in the discussion of the Golden Rule. So on that basis, Art should avoid participation in the monitoring. On the other hand, anyone seduced into drug use is surely being harmed; stopping the drug dealing would reduce or eliminate that effect. From that standpoint, facilitating the monitoring might be ethically defensible.

1.7 Respect the privacy of others

As stated above, innocent computer users, as well as the guilty, have their privacy violated by the monitoring.

3.   Organizational Leadership Imperatives

As an ACM member and an organizational leader, I will . . .

3.2 Manage personnel and resources to design and build information systems that enhance the quality of working life

Monitoring without knowledge and permission, it may be argued, does not enhance the quality of working life of those monitored. Sooner or later, facts or even rumors about the monitoring will surface. The outcome could include any number of results, fear and resentment among them.

3.3 Acknowledge and support proper and authorized uses of an organization's computing and communication resources

This imperative summarizes Art Betony's dilemma. Is the monitoring a *proper* and *authorized* use of the computing resource? If policy allows it, the monitoring may be authorized, but that is only half the requirement. The use must also be proper to justify Art's support. Thus the code is not helpful in labeling this action as either proper or improper.

3.5 Articulate and support policies that protect the dignity of users and others affected by a computing system

It could be argued that monitoring without permission or knowledge does not protect dignity, that it shows disrespect for the individual. Article 3.5 would thus support Art in not providing the software to Alberta Wilson.

In summary, Art's reference to the ACM code still leaves him with the ethical problem unsolved. There is a strong argument in favor of monitoring—to foster human well-being—but some imperatives support the opposing view of respecting privacy. Finally, some imperatives, such as Article 3.3, represent worthwhile objectives, but do not contribute to the solution directly.

The final guideline asks, does the action violate the Golden Rule? In other words, Art must ask himself if he would want this done to him. Would he want his work monitored without his knowledge or permission? Some might answer that they have nothing to hide, and therefore such monitoring would be acceptable. Others might argue that although they have nothing to hide, some actions could be misinterpreted, and thus they would object to monitoring. For example, suppose the person being monitored is creating a word processing document, and the observer monitoring that activity sees hardly any words being keyed. The observer might conclude that the worker is lazy or inefficient. The worker, however, is actually composing a major market analysis and consulting numerous source documents. Thus, research time is interspersed with the typing. In the Califon case, it appears that the Golden Rule does not give Art a conclusive answer.

At this point, it is clear to Art that there is an ethical dilemma. His informal analysis, however, has not defined his dilemma with very much precision nor has it given him a specific course of action. Art must now move to an examination of ethical principles and the application of the four-step process.

USING THE FOUR-STEP PROCESS

This commentary will follow the four-step process for ethical analysis and decision making (Figure 3-1) to reach a conclusion about the sample case.

Each element of the process will be broken into three parts. The first part will explain the structure of the process and the rationale for the particular step being executed. The second part will present the authors' ethical analysis of the sample case in the form of a worksheet entry. This will also illustrate how the worksheets in Appendix B are used to organize the process responses. The third section will discuss how the authors arrived at the ethical analysis.

Step I. Understanding the situation

IA. List and number the relevant facts.

Process Structure

Step IA may seem simplistic and unnecessary. Yet great confusion and wasted effort can result if all parties do not understand the situation the same way and agree on the facts. It need not take long, but Step IA is essential.

The case study presents many facts, some more relevant than others. Stating these facts should be, as much as possible, a neutral, logical exercise. Although interpretation is involved in selecting pertinent facts, do not judge them in this step. Comments such as "Clare should not have viewed anyone's screen without their permission" are inappropriate here. The fact that Clare "roves electronically," however, must be noted. Facts that raise ethical questions will be further handled in Step IB.

Another value to listing the relevant facts is to discover what we don't know. We never have all the information we need when making decisions. Sometimes we can afford to spend the time and other resources to find out more. But at some point, we must make decisions based on whatever information we have on hand. Lack of information is not an excuse for deferring action. Decision makers must be willing to make a choice based on the current facts, and must possess the courage to reevaluate that choice and, perhaps, change it when new facts become known.

Worksheet Entry
Step IA. List and number the relevant facts.

Number	Fact
1	Califon is a distributor of electronic equipment, with a large in-house computer system supporting more than 100 users.
2	Clare Valerian is a Califon technical-support person who helps end-users with their computer problems.
3	Clare has a new utility program, LANSCAPE, that enables her to duplicate on her screen exactly what is taking place on a user's screen.

4	LANSCAPE allows Clare to "rove electronically," that is, to view, without their permission, what people are doing on their computers.
5	LANSCAPE enables Clare to avoid having to go to the user to solve a problem, resulting in greater efficiency and more satisfied users.
6	Clare recommends continued use of LANSCAPE and suggests making it available to others in her group who perform similar troubleshooting activities.
7	Art Betony, V.P. for Information Systems, is so impressed with LANSCAPE that he describes its success to Alberta Wilson, Califon Executive V.P.
8	Alberta reveals that there may be a drug-dealing operation at Califon.
9	Alberta tells Art of other surveillance attempts.
10	Alberta asks for LANSCAPE on her terminal so she can monitor the computer activities of the suspected drug dealers.
11	Art Betony makes no immediate commitment.

Discussion

We could perhaps add other "facts," such as the Califon chain of command. Or, it may be argued that some of the "facts" listed are really value judgments or opinions and should be deleted in favor of purely objective statements. For example, the statement that Clare was "roving electronically" without permission is in one sense a fact, but in another sense a judgment about Clare's actions. Thus, an argument could be made to leave it off the list in Step IA. If you take that position, be sure Clare's "rovings" are included in Step IB and the discussion in Step IV.

The best approach for the sake of completeness is to list *all* facts in Step IA, referring to some of them again in Step IB. If it makes sense to distinguish "subjective" from "objective" facts, label them appropriately. What this step is trying to answer is, "What is the subject of this case?" or "What is it all about?" Of course, these questions have a variety of answers, but the answers should be simple. Longer answers tend to bring in the reasons for the actions, which belong in Steps III or IV. In this case, the answers must reflect the facts that LANSCAPE allows one person to monitor what others are doing at their computers without their knowledge; that LANSCAPE is a useful tool for technical-support personnel; that the Executive V.P. thinks there is drug dealing at Califon; and that the Executive V.P. wants to use LANSCAPE to monitor employee computer use to find the drug dealers.

IB. Which of these raises an ethical issue? Why? What is the potential or resulting harm?

Process Structure

As mentioned earlier, ethical dilemmas are composed of multiple issues, which must be "peeled" like an onion. Some issues are more important than others. Some issues must be resolved before others. At this stage in the analysis, it is important to look at the facts as we know them and indicate which ones raise ethical questions and give some reason why we feel that way. A complete ethical analysis is not called for. We will do that later for the major ethical issue.

Worksheet Entry
Step IB.   Which of these raises an ethical issue? Why? What is the potential or resulting harm?
Fact (number)   *Potential or resulting harm*

Fact	Potential or resulting harm
4	Users not informed of "roving," privacy question
8	Illegal activity, drug users and company harmed
9	Was this (another) invasion of privacy?
10	Is this fair to all concerned?

Discussion

In almost any ethical situation, multiple contributory actions occuring over a period of time lead to a crisis situation or, as it is sometimes called, "the moment of truth," when a decision must be made. Step IB is designed to peel away those contributory actions to expose the "real" issue or, more precisely, the issue to be dealt with now. Usually the contributory actions have already happened, and it is their effect that is being felt at present. We may wish they had not happened, and may subsequently have to confront the perpetrators of those actions, but at the moment, we have to deal with their effects.

In this case, fact 4 (Clare looks at users' screens without their knowledge or permission), although a questionable act, is not the major issue at this moment. Fact 8's assertion of drug dealing, if true, could be problematic in a number of ways. People who abuse drugs will continue to be harmed, the company's reputation may suffer if word gets out, and worker productivity could diminish if the drugs are taken on the job. This, too, is not the primary issue, but rather a serious contributing factor to the dilemma. Fact 9 raises the issue of appropriate measures. We don't know how Alberta performed her previous monitoring, and it may be that rights were violated and the actions were not justified. However, these past actions do not need to be addressed immediately.

Fact 10 points to the real issue, the "moment of truth," altough it does not express it directly. But because of the other actions we have considered, Alberta's request raises similar questions of privacy invasion, users' rights, and the necessity to respond to the suspected drug dealing.

Some may suggest that other questionable actions, or other reasons for a questionable action, could be added to Step IB. This is certainly possible. However, the reasons in this step are expected to be cursory and not a full ethical analysis. We are only interested in an elementary justification for the inclusion of a given action.

As to whether every action should be included, the rule is the same as for including relevant facts. When in doubt, include the action. For example, you might want to include fact 11 (Art makes no immediate comment). Doesn't Art have a duty to obey his superior? Is it ethical for him to hesitate? The main objective of Step IB is to list enough questionable actions so the current issue becomes clear. We'll come back to this in Step II. At this time, however, we must agree on one further set of facts that will aid in the analysis. We need to ask, who are the stakeholders?

IC. List the stakeholders involved.

Process Structure

Listing the stakeholders is a key task in this analysis because it helps to determine who is affected by the action. Often, this part of the exercise generates some surprises. Sometimes, just realizing that someone is a stakeholder influences the solution and recommendations. Later, in Step IVC, we will test our conclusions by examining how these stakeholders are affected by the decisions we have made.

Worksheet Entry
Step IC. List the stakeholders involved.
Clare
The Director of User Support
Art Betony, V.P. Information Systems (and his family)
Alberta Wilson, Executive V.P.
The other technical-support people
All computer users at Califon
The suspected drug dealers
The drug users, customers of the dealers
Califon as a corporation
All Califon employees

Califon stockholders
Califon customers
Society as a whole
The producers of LANSCAPE
Other LANSCAPE users

Discussion

A judgment must be made whether a stakeholder is important enough to be listed. There may be a number of secondary or fringe stakeholders, and including them and their claims might not contribute much to the solution. In this case, one could argue that other users of LANSCAPE are stakeholders because any misuse of that software or bad publicity it receives might have implications for them. But such an occurrence, should it happen, is clearly not central to the issue. Fringe stakeholders might be listed for the sake of thoroughness or as a way of accounting for all concerned parties, but it is a waste of time to spend any further effort on those whose interests have no significant bearing on the outcomes.

Step II. Isolating the major ethical dilemma

What is the ethical dilemma to be resolved NOW? State it using the form: Should **someone** do or not do **something**? Note: Just state the dilemma here; leave any reasoning for Step III.

Process Structure

This is where the true focus of the case is clearly expressed. Solving this dilemma is the major task. Choosing the right issue, and having participants in the process agree on what that issue is, is so important that this action is given its own separate step.

The way the issue is expressed is also important to its analysis and resolution. An issue, by definition, implies controversy and more than one point of view. Simply saying that the issue in this case is "privacy" or "the employee's right to privacy" is not sufficient. Privacy and privacy rights are only aspects of the issue. What is it about privacy that is being questioned? It is whether or not it is being violated. Hence, an issue is best presented in the form of a question so that the resolution is the answer to that question.

We suggest posing a question in the form, "Should **someone** do or not do **something**? " The present tense is used because we are focusing on the current "moment of truth," not on past contributory actions. Secondly, the format requires identification of an actor and an action. This focuses the ethical analysis. It is *this* actor and *this* action that is to be evaluated. The actor can be a person or, more generally, a corporate "person." If we don't know who the responsible individual is, it is appropriate at this point to enter in Step II words like "the organization" or "management," for example, "Should LANSCAPE management have issued its software without a privacy warning?"

Though the question is simple and refers to one actor and one action, dilemmas with multiple actors and actions are accommodated through the analysis in Step III, especially when considering rights and duties, and throughout Step IV. Finally, any ethical reasoning should be left to Step III. There is no need to justify or explain the Step II entry.

Worksheet Entry
Step II. Isolating the major ethical dilemma What is the ethical dilemma to be resolved NOW? Should Art provide LANSCAPE software to Alberta so she can monitor computer activities in an attempt to discover suspected drug dealers?

Discussion

This is the major dilemma for Art now. However, as described in Step IB, other dilemmas and contributing factors will influence him. Some are: Should Alberta Wilson monitor employee computer use without their knowledge or consent? (This is really one aspect of the major dilemma.) Should Clare have done her electronic roving without the knowledge and consent of her users? (A contributory factor, but not central now.) Should Califon management have established a policy on computer monitoring prior to implementing LANSCAPE? (A contributory factor, but not central now.) Should Alberta have told Art Betony about the suspected drug dealing? (A contributory factor, but not central now.) Should Art refuse the request of his superior? (One aspect of the major dilemma for Art.) Some of these issues are more important than others. But the minor issues should not be overlooked, as they often provide insights into attitudes or actions that contribute to the solutions and recommendations. In this case, the central question is whether to give Alberta the software.

Step III. Analyzing the ethicality of both alternatives in Step II

Step III takes the most time and discussion. This is appropriate, since without fully understanding the ethical issues, a quality decision cannot be achieved. In Step III, ethical analysis is performed through responding to a set of questions that have at their core a number of commonly held ethical principles. The answers to the questions do not give the "ethical solution," but do provide insight into how a given principle applies to the situation. The individual still must synthesize all the responses and draw his or her own conclusions based on personal judgment. The purpose, however, is to provide supporting reasoning for whatever conclusion is drawn. This part of the process provides the ethical defense for that conclusion.

Step III is divided into three major sections representing consequentialism, rights and duties, and Kant's categorical imperative.

Consequentialism

Process Structure

Each question should be read using a consistent form of the action in Step II. For instance, item A below might be read, "If *Art gives LANSCAPE to Alberta,* who, if anyone, will be harmed?" Usually the names of the individuals are a sufficient response, but sometimes the nature or magnitude of the result is helpful. Thus, the response for A includes the fact that innocent computer users would experience potential privacy violations. It is possible that no one will be affected or that some aspect of the ethical principle does not apply to the question. In these cases, "no one" or "not applicable" are appropriate entries.

Worksheet Entry

Step III. Analyzing the ethicality of both alternatives in Step II
Consequentialism

A. If action in Step II is done, who, if anyone, will be harmed?

   Innocent computer users' privacy is violated, drug dealers may get caught

B. If action in Step II is not done, who, if anyone, will be harmed?

   Those newly "hooked" on drugs and current addicts continue to get supplied; Califon may suffer through low productivity, possible accidents, and bad reputation, resulting in negative effects for employees, stockholders, customers.

C. Which alternative results in the least harm, A or B?

   A

D. If action in Step II is done, who, if anyone, will benefit?

   All employees, those who would be "hooked," Califon, customers (better product), society (if dealers are caught)

E. If action in Step II is not done, who, if anyone, will benefit?

   Drug dealers, current drug users, innocent computer users

F. Which alternative results in the maximum benefit, D or E?

   E

Discussion

At this point we have some insights into the harm and benefits that may result from giving or not giving Alberta the software. In a sense, we are performing a cost-benefit analysis, weighing the amount of benefit and harm from a given action. How weights are applied will influence the answer. It may be misleading to simply use the numbers of people involved as the criterion.

For example, certainly more people will be potentially harmed if Art does not give Alberta the software than will be harmed if he does give it to her. Yet that is not the whole story. Other factors have to be weighed and included in the equation before an entry is made in section C. How important is privacy? What is the likelihood of this situation becoming a problem for customers, employees, and stockholders? How an individual judges each of the entries in the equation determines which response is entered in C, and later in F. In the preceding sample analysis, privacy rights of innocent computer users were given strong emphasis in A and E, tipping the scales in that direction. So even though there were large numbers of people benefitting in B and D, and even though drug dealers and users seem to get a break, the authors reasoned that A and E were the most desirable conditions.

Rights and Duties

IIIG. What rights have been or may be abridged? What duties have been or may be neglected? Identify the stakeholder and the right or duty. When listing a right, show its corresponding duty and vice versa.

Process Structure

The entries expected here are explained in detail in Chapter 1. Analysis can start with a right that is not being respected or a duty that is not being met. Either way, the corresponding right or duty is discovered next. There are numerous rights and duties in any situation. It is important to isolate those that are relevant to the issue in Step II.

Worksheet Entry

Step III. Analyzing the ethicality of both alternatives in Step II

Rights and Duties

G. What rights have been or may be abridged? What duties have been or may be neglected?

1. Employees have a **right** to know they are monitored. Califon has a **duty** to tell them.

2. Califon has a **right** to protect its assets and reputation. Employees have a **duty** not to inhibit productivity/quality by drug use.

3. Art, as an employee, has a **duty** to serve Califon, principally Alberta, his boss. Alberta has a **duty** not to ask Art to do something that may violate his principles.

4. Califon has a **duty** to protect its employees. Employees have a **right** to a safe (drug-free) workplace.

5. Clare has a **duty** to explain the monitoring function of LANSCAPE to her users. This is a question of *trust*, *integrity*, and *truthfulness* emanating from her *professional relationship* with the users. She, as the professional, has superior knowledge, and has the *responsibility* to see that those without that level of knowledge are not *harmed* as a result. The users have a **right** to expect this behavior.

Discussion

Other rights and duties may apply here, but these exemplify the ones that bear directly on the issue. Note that certain sets of rights and duties are in conflict. For example, the employees' right to know they are monitored inhibits Califon's ability to protect its assets by discovering the drug dealers. Such conflicts are resolved in a manner similar to the answers in the consequentialism section, by weighing one against the other and making a judgment.

In item 3 above, although only duties are mentioned, the rights of each to expect such behavior are implied. We consider this kind of intuitive leap a sign of more mature analysis. It occurs when one skips over more obvious associations and arrives at the more subtle and relevant relationships. Item 3 above could have been more explicitly stated as:

3A. Art has a **duty** to serve Alberta, his boss. Alberta has a **right** to request his help.

3B. Alberta has a **duty** not to ask Art to do something that violates his principles. Art has a **right** to refuse such a request.

Kant's Categorical Imperative

Process Structure

The approach here corresponds to the consequentialism section, in that questions are formulated to reflect various aspects of Kant's categorical imperative. Again, a principle may not apply, or in a given situation no one may be affected. For example, in K below, if Art gives LANSCAPE to Alberta, all users will be treated alike; they will be monitored. Thus, achieving that consistency does not necessarily contribute to an ethical solution.

Worksheet Entry

Step III. Analyzing the ethicality of both alternatives in Step II
Kant's Categorical Imperative

H. If action in Step II is done, who, if anyone, will be treated with *disre*-spect?

Innocent computer users

I. If action in Step II is not done, who, if anyone, will be treated with *disre*-spect?

No one

J. Which alternative is preferable, H or I?

I

K. If action in Step II is done, who, if anyone, will be treated *un*like others?

No one

L. If action in Step II is not done, who, if anyone, will be treated *un*like others?

No one

M. Which alternative is preferable, K or L?

Neither

N. Are there benefits if everyone did action in Step II? (In other words, would we want everyone to be monitored or everyone to be able to monitor another at will?)

No. It would violate everyone's privacy.

O. Are there benefits if nobody did action in Step II?

Yes, privacy protected.

P. Which alternative is preferable, N or O?

O

Discussion

After considering and discussing arguments and principles, it is necessary to weigh them and draw conclusions. In this case, the issue boils down to user privacy rights versus the public good of apprehending drug dealers and the corporate good of the intrinsic value of LANSCAPE. The authors believe that the right to privacy and the issues of permission and informed consent to the monitoring outweigh the need to discover the drug dealers. In some circumstances, rights may be legitimately set aside or limited, especially when other rights may be at stake. For example, invasion of privacy may be justified to prevent greater harm, as when someone breaks into a locked dorm room from which smoke is discovered coming under the door. The need to put out the fire, and perhaps save a life, overrides the privacy right.

Based on what we know in this case, it is not clear whether preventing the greater harm (drug dealing) will really be achieved. We have no idea of the extent of the drug operation, if any; how much harm it is doing, if any; how much risk of harm it presents to Califon and its employees; how sure Alberta is that the drug dealing exists; what chance she has of actually finding the culprits; how admissible the evidence acquired from the monitoring will be; what the law enforcement authorities have to do with this; and what the CEO and Board of Directors feel, or whether they are informed at all.

Furthermore, we have no idea of what harm will be caused to innocent people who are included in the monitoring. Nor do we know whether such monitoring will stop after the drug bust. Suppose the drug dealers are not using the computer to help them? How far and for how long will the search be expanded before this is discovered?

It makes no difference that Alberta previously performed other forms of surveillance. Those actions may have been illegal and unethical. It also makes no difference that Art is Alberta's subordinate. His duty to the organization and other stakeholders overrides his relationship with Alberta. Of course, as a practical matter, he may lose his job or suffer other harm, which has implications for his duty to self and family. But that is not sufficient reason for him to violate his responsibility as a computer professional and act unethically. Thus, in this case, G1, H, and O outweigh the other entries, and Art should refuse to allow Alberta to use LANSCAPE as she proposes. We can now enter this conclusion in Step IVA.

Step IV. Making a decision and planning the implementation

IVA. Make a defensible ethical decision.

Based on the analysis in Step III, respond to the question in Step II. Indicate the letters of the categories that best support your response. Add any arguments justifying your choice of these ethical principles to support your decision. Where there are conflicting rights and duties, choose and defend those that take precedence. (Note: Just make and justify your choice here; leave any action steps for parts B and D, which follow.)

Process Structure

Step IV is essential for placing the situation in a real context, for moving from principles to practices. The justification and supporting arguments are what bring quality to the ethical decision. Disagreements among decision makers can be discussed through arguing principles rather than through emotion or personal biases. Furthermore, isolating principles provides an avenue for generalizing the specific conclusion in the case to similar situations as they arise.

Worksheet Entry

Step IVA. Make a defensible ethical decision.

Based on the analysis in Step III, respond to the question in Step II.

Art should not provide LANSCAPE to Alberta without further information (see Step IVB below). G1, H, O The right to privacy and treating users with respect are more important than catching drug dealers, especially since the likelihood of this succeeding is slim.

Discussion

There may be other remedies to this situation that do not require anyone to act unethically. Making defensible ethical decisions may leave us feeling uncomfortable. Perhaps we have not tied up all the loose ends or some harm results from the choice we make, even though it appears the best choice possible. Ethical choices are not made with absolute certainty; they are not deductive like mathematical problems and solutions. Ethical decisions are made through judgment and by validating that judgment through a rational appeal to principles. The danger is in not acting at all, in never making a decision or judgment. As the axiom says, "Not to act, is to act." Failing to act will simply allow a wrongful situation to continue or get worse. The best you can do is be aware of the opposing positions, make the decision on the available facts, and as facts and circumstances change, have the courage to defend or change your decision.

We have made a choice, what we see as the lesser of two evils. A lot could still go wrong, but that should not change the choice. What is required is a thorough response in Step IVB.

IVB. List the specific steps needed to implement your defensible ethical decision.

Process Structure

The discovery of the potential harm or neglected duties or people being mistreated is synthesized to arrive at a defensible ethical decision. But knowing what to do and deciding how to do it are two completely different things. Awareness of harm, duties, or mistreatment, however, can guide us to implementation steps that take those factors into account, and deal with them.

Worksheet Entry

Step IVB. List the specific steps needed to implement your defensible ethical decision.

1. Art meets with Alberta and explains the importance of privacy rights and the potential for damaging morale, lowering productivity, and setting a bad precedent. Together they plan an ethical response.

2. Publish a policy that, at a minimum, announces to all users and potential users how LANSCAPE works.

3. Only then, perhaps, install LANSCAPE for Alberta, since users will now use it with informed consent.

4. Engage law enforcement help in apprehending the drug dealers.

5. Be prepared to defend the ethical decision should the drug dealing become public or other calamity happen.

Discussion

Art and Alberta might decide to involve top management, perhaps even the Board of Directors. They must answer the questions raised in Step III: Is there a policy governing monitoring? What previous type of surveillance has taken place? Who knew about it? Was it legal? Were law enforcement authorities involved? Just how serious is the risk to Califon? How many people are involved? What is the basis of the suspicion of drug dealing? What is the likelihood of discovering sufficient evidence for arrest and conviction? These answers will put the problem in better perspective and may lead to further questions and suggestions for action.

At the very least, a top-level policy decision on monitoring should result. Such a policy might state that the computer resource is owned by Califon and is to be used for Califon business. Further, it could state that no presumption of privacy should be made by those using the system. As an example, or as a special section, the use and full capability of LANSCAPE could be explained.

Publishing the policy would put all users on notice, would satisfy the knowledge requirement, and might provide the ethical justification for some limited monitoring to discover the drug dealers. The drug dealers could react in two ways. They could take the publication of the policy casually, as just another memo to be filed. In that case, they might well be caught through the monitoring. Or, if they took the memo seriously, they would stop using the computer for their activities. This might diminish or end their ability to operate at Califon or force them to operate in a more open manner, which may lead to their discovery. In other words, being open and ethical about the potential for monitoring might very well have the same result as being covert and unethical.

IVC. Show how the major stakeholders are affected by these actions.

Process Structure

This is a checkpoint. Evaluating how each stakeholder is affected shows what harms are still possible and what value the decision has brought. This guides implementation decisions and reduces surprises during the implementation phase.

Worksheet Entry
Step IVC. Show how the major stakeholders are affected by these actions. 1. Clare now acts "openly." 2. The Director of User Support can now proliferate use of LANSCAPE without compounding the problem. 3. Art and Alberta fulfill their duties to the users, Califon, and each other. 4. The other technical support people can use LANSCAPE properly. 5. Computer users and their privacy are respected. 6. Perhaps drug dealers and users are apprehended in spite of informing users of the possibility of monitoring through LANSCAPE. 7. Califon, all its customers, employees, and stockholders are assured of a quality product and avoid the threat of bad publicity and other dire consequences. 8. Society as a whole will benefit from increased privacy protection, but may suffer should the drug dealers not be caught. 9. The producers and other users of LANSCAPE can benefit from this experience and avoid similar dilemmas.

Discussion

Most of the effects appear to be positive. The one serious danger is that it will be business as usual for the drug dealers.

IVD. What other longer-term changes (political, legal, technical, societal, organizational) would help prevent such problems in the future?

Process Structure

This step asks you to apply your knowledge of organizations, politics, the legislative process, technology, and society to suggest broad, global, long-term solutions to prevent this kind of situation from happening again. You might also consider:

What organizational support structures or obstacles exist, and what might be needed?

Can (additional) disclosure, communication, or compromise resolve the issue or prevent recurrence? How can this be done?

Worksheet Entry

Step IVD. What other, longer-term changes would help prevent such problems in the future?

1. Foster an ethical corporate culture at Califon so that people like Clare, Art, and Alberta can become sensitive to ethical situations.

2. Develop a code of ethics, teach it, and reward adherence to it. Such an initiative often benefits the company in the form of a good reputation that is marketable.

3. Establish an ethics hotline at Califon, a free phone number or some other way of reporting unethical activity. This should include any unethical activity, not just unethical activities involving computers. Through such a vehicle, Clare's roving might have been reported and the drug dealers might even have been exposed.

4. Enact state or federal statutes to protect workers who are monitored. (Legal solutions, however, often require a long time and great expense.)

Discussion

Each of these suggestions requires further discussion and analysis. This could amount to a comprehensive feasibility study that might include gathering more data about the proposed activity, performing a cost-benefit analysis, preparing an ethical impact statement, and drafting an implementation plan.

IVE. What should have been done or not done in the first place (at the pivot point) to avoid this dilemma?

Process Structure

Identifying pivot points is valuable for sensitizing individuals to the early-warning signs of an ethical situation. The earlier an ethical dilemma is discovered, the easier it is to solve, since there will be fewer layers to the problem.

Finding the pivot points after the fact is one way to discover corrective measures. Where could the situation have "turned around" if only someone had done something differently?

Worksheet Entry

Step IVE. What should have been done or not done in the first place to avoid this dilemma?

1. A policy decision was needed when the decision was made to perform Alberta's original surveillance.

2. An ethical impact study was needed of how LANSCAPE was to be used when it was first purchased.

Discussion

If the privacy issues had been faced at the time of the original surveillance, that could have helped with the LANSCAPE problem. Had there been prior thought about the consequences of LANSCAPE use, Clare may not have been free to rove, users may have been more explicitly informed, and Alberta's request may never have arisen.

Other risks arise from not having an explicit privacy policy. One of the users might have been offended by Clare's roving without permission and could have reported it to another manager or even revealed it outside the company. Or, suppose Clare, in her roving, had discovered some improper computer use—game playing, for instance, or even the drug dealing? Without a policy or some supporting structure, she would have had no guidance in responding to these situations.

A Way to Expand the Analysis

Sometimes in Step III, or after Step IV, it is worthwhile to alter some of the parameters in the case to see if different circumstances change the analysis and perhaps lead to different outcomes. This helps to discover variables that might be controllable and hence could be part of the short- and long-term solutions. The following questions display one approach for altering parameters. They all take the form "Does it matter that . . . ." The authors' responses are in brackets.

- Does it matter that Califon was an electronics company and not in some other industry? [No. Its obligation is the same no matter what the industry.]

- Does it matter that Alberta is a woman? [No. This is not a gender-based issue.]

- Does it matter that the offense is drug dealing and not something else, like game playing? [Yes. If it were a minor offense like game playing, a memo or bulletin board posting may have been sufficient.]

- Does it matter that the producers of LANSCAPE may have had no intention of their program being used in this way? [Probably not, unless there was something in the license agreement. But perhaps they should have done an ethical analysis as they were developing the software and then put a warning label on the product.]

- Does it matter that Califon had no policy on computer monitoring? [It sure does. This was explained in an earlier section.]

- Does it matter that LANSCAPE produced enormous productivity gains? [No. This fact does not change the ethicality of covert surveillance.]

- Does it matter that Alberta sanctioned other forms of surveillance previously? [Yes. We need to know more about this because it is not clear whether this was an appropriate action.]

- Does it matter that the surveillance utility was designed specifically to be used in such a way that the user was unaware of its operation? [No. Just the existence of a functionality does not justify its use without considering other factors in the situation.]

Another question that should always be included is: If you could do it all over again, what would you do differently? In this case, one response to that question might be that Califon should have had some sort of corporate anti-drug campaign and policy that might have prevented the necessity for any of this. If the company had been vigilant early on, the drug dealing might never have started.

SUMMARY

As we demonstrated through the analysis of the sample case, ethical problems comprise many layers. To make and implement sound ethical decisions, you must understand all the facts. The stronger positions are those supported by ethical principles. Short- and long-term resolutions are not easy to develop or implement.

You are now ready to solve cases and make ethically defensible decisions on your own; that is, you will be able to give principled reasons for the decisions you reach.

Part

2

The Cases

The real-life cases presented in Part II reflect a variety of computer-related circumstances that call for ethical decision making. Many are based on the experiences of information systems professionals; others are based on the authors' own experiences and research.

Each case contains a number of factors. There are often multiple ethical issues, overlapping situations, and different personalities. And, as in real life, there are confounding circumstances and extraneous facts that must be weeded out.

After using the process recommended in Chapter 3 to read and discuss a number of cases, you should be able to:

- Distinguish the relevant facts of a case and discover the stakeholders— that is, those who have an interest, or stake, in the outcome.

- Discover the facts that are ethical issues and their potential for harm.

- Identify the primary issue to be resolved now.

- Analyze the ethicality of the alternatives and apply ethical principles to make a defensible ethical decision.

- Suggest a course of action to resolve the current situation.

- Recommend long-term systemic, organizational, or societal policies and strategies to prevent a similar situation in the future.

Case

1

Levity or Libel?

An E-Mail–Based Effort to Boost Morale Backfires

The LowRider Tractor Corporation had a reputation for manufacturing heavy-duty earth-moving equipment. Its Military Division produced more tank turrets, hulls, and suspensions than any other contractor. For many years, the Military Division sustained the corporation by its aggressive marketing of military hardware overseas. During the late 1980s and early 1990s, however, the Military Division experienced decreased orders for tank parts. Because LowRider was so dependent on tank hardware revenues, management was faced with the task of significantly reducing the workforce.

The Board of Directors of LowRider had never experienced such tough economic times. The directors issued a memorandum, which called for a reorganization to reduce the payroll in each division by 10 percent over a six-month period. The severity and speed of the cut left little room for compromise. In some departments, workers were laid off without consideration of the value or length of their service at LowRider. The drastic downsizing was certain to cause resentment and ill will.

At LowRider's world headquarters in New Hope, Nebraska, Bill Brundle worked as a software engineer. He designed and installed graphics modeling programs. His department had suffered its share of cuts, and it seemed to everyone that the workload was greater than ever. Employee morale was at an all-time low.

In Bill's eyes, what his department needed was a good laugh, preferably at the company's expense. Maybe that would boost morale. He approached the department's test data designer, Betty Hastings, who was his closest friend and confidante. He told her about his idea for distributing a document that would be good for a laugh. Betty thought it was a grand idea and even offered to help, but Bill said he preferred to work alone.

Bill spent an entire evening at his terminal, composing a memo mocking the reorganization. This memo poked fun at the upper levels of management and contained some slang four-letter words. After composing the memo and signing it "Management," Bill distributed it through e-mail to all workers in the department. Due to his knowledge of software engineering, he could bypass the system security software and send the memo anonymously.

The effect of the memo was immediate. Several people in Bill's department e-mailed it to other departments, and it traveled throughout the company. It was the sole topic of conversation at all gatherings. People laughed at some phrasings and wandered from one office to another to share discovered double meanings. A few workers blushed at some of the words, and some said, "I just don't find it funny." But because so many co-workers enjoyed it, Bill sensed success. When asked who wrote it, however, he said he didn't know. Betty also said nothing, though of course she knew who had written it. The memo was reprinted and copied, and it continued to spread like fire in dry grass.

Eventually, the division director, Harriet Corrigan, got a copy. Harriet didn't like the memo at all. It was difficult enough to reduce the size of the division without what she called "this kind of insensitive criticism." Harriet promptly ordered technicians to identify the workstation from which the memo originated. They had no difficulty identifying the source, and when Harriet confronted Bill, he freely admitted his actions.

Harriet is concerned. Should she fire Bill? Bill's job is crucial to the division, and Harriet would be obliged to replace him immediately. However, Betty Hastings could do Bill's job, and this would be fortunate for Betty because her position as test data designer is due to be eliminated by the reorganization.

2

Credit Woes

A Credit Bureau Faces a Decision of Whether to Revise a System

Annabelle and Arvin Dorland made an offer on a three-bedroom house in Grande Pointe, New Hampshire. The sellers accepted the offer, and everything seemed to be going well. The home was their dream house, with all the features they ever wanted.

Jenny Cartier works for First Fiduciary Trust, the bank through which the Dorlands applied for their mortgage. With the Dorlands' permission, Jenny asked for a credit report from Canyon Credit Company. Canyon is one of three major nationwide credit bureaus.

After an uneventful but anxious three days, the Dorlands received a phone call from Jenny at the bank. She said that the credit report from Canyon showed that the Dorlands had an outstanding lien on a fishing boat in Happy Jack, Louisiana. For that reason, the bank couldn't approve their mortgage application. Arvin was incensed. He told Jenny that there had to be a mistake—that neither he nor Annabelle had ever even visited Louisiana, much less bought a boat there.

Jenny replied that if the Dorlands wanted their dream house and a First Fiduciary mortgage, they'd better get the problem cleared up fast. Another couple wanted to make an offer on the house, and the seller wouldn't wait more than 48 hours. Jenny gave Arvin the name and phone number of Louise Patella, her contact at Canyon Credit.

U.S. law allows anyone to get the details of his or her credit report and suggest corrections. Arvin immediately contacted Louise. She researched the problem and discovered another Arvin Dorland, a man from Magnolia, Louisiana. Louise realized that the company had two different Arvin Dorlands on file—the Arvin in New Hampshire was in his mid-30s, while the Arvin in Louisiana was 72. By the time Louise corrected the database and issued a new report to First Fiduciary, the Dorlands' dream house had been sold to someone else.

Arvin and Annabelle's concern is that the bank will always associate the Dorlands with "that problem with the boat in Louisiana." Also, they worry that the other two credit companies the bank uses could distribute the erroneous information.

Louise's husband, Peter, also works at Canyon Credit. Peter is the director of systems analysis and design, and he and Louise have often discussed the increasing frequency of complaints concerning incorrect credit reports. After hearing about the Dorlands' problem, he approached the chief information officer (CIO) of Canyon Credit to suggest a change in the database. Peter argued that the simple coding scheme used to identify a record for retrieval worked fine when the database was small. But now that the database system was large, it needed to be modified so all records could be more easily and correctly accessed. Such a change would allow growth to one billion records and eliminate the mistaken-identity problem.

The CIO directed Peter to do a full cost-benefit analysis of the matter. Peter discovered that to convert to using unique numeric identifiers would cost over $720,000 and save the company $90,000 per year. Some savings would result from the elimination of claims processing where clients were misidentified. Even larger savings could be realized from reductions in court settlements to those adversely affected by the system's errors. Peter concluded that the gain in reputation and increased customer satisfaction would be enough to justify the change. The CIO, on the other hand, considered the errors in the database a small problem. Based on the high initial cost and the long payback period shown by the cost-benefit analysis, he was against the change. The dispute was reported to the Information Systems Steering Committee for resolution.

Case

3

Narrative
Version

Something for Everyone

Recombination of Data at a Supermarket

On Elm Street in Happy Valley, Massachusetts, Mary Smith returns from the mailbox, sorting the day's arrivals. Her husband, John, is trimming the hedge.

"John, look! We got a coupon in the mail! It's a fifteen-dollar discount to have our dog Rover groomed. How did they know?"

"Know what?"

"Well, how did Molly's Pet Grooming Service know we have a dog? Do you suppose one of our neighbors told them about Rover?"

"Mary, I can't see how that's likely. It must be one of those hit-or-miss mass mailings. Anyway, let's use that coupon. It sure is a good deal."

At Chambord's Supermarket administrative offices in Griffin, Massachusetts, Nola Brickell, Information Systems Administrator for the 12-store Chambord chain, talks with her boss, General Manager Pierre Nadeau.

"Pierre, do you remember Molly Graubert, that sweet old woman who asked us if we could sell her a list of pet owners?"

"Yeah? So what does she want now?" Pierre remembers how easy it was to get that list. All customers who pay by check use Chambord's ID cards, which cross-index to their addresses. The checkout scanners log the customers' purchases, duplicating the sales receipts, with details on everything they buy. The receipts include the ID number. All Nola had to do to create the list Molly wanted was to ask the computer for the names and addresses of all people who bought pet food or pet supplies. True, that list didn't include the buyers who paid with cash, but it met Molly's needs.

"Well," said Nola, "I've had three different calls from people who found out about us selling Molly that list. The head of marketing at Relaxed Retirement, the mail-order outfit that sells the Florida condos, wants a list of the people who buy old-age health stuff—you know, denture cream, corn plasters, and such."

"Yeah, so? Who else called?"

"Mr. Campbell, the head of sales at Farwell Auto, asked for a list of the customers who bought maps, vacation-planning guides, and motor oil. I guess he's looking for people who might be in the market for a new car. And here's a strange one: Brumble's Department Store wanted a list of our customers who didn't buy any frozen foods for two weeks in a row. He figured that they wouldn't have a freezer. I told them all no way, of course. But I thought you should know."

Mr. Nadeau is visibly angry. "Hey, Nola, why'd you do that? Do you realize how much money there is in those lists? And it's free money, too. I mean, you can create those lists with no trouble at all, right? Am I right?" He's almost shouting.

"Yes, but . . . It's not right."

"Not right? What do you mean, not right?"

"Well, it's not . . . it just doesn't seem right."

"Hey, Nola, get off it. We feel good making forty cents on a bag of groceries, and you're telling me it's not right to improve our profit picture? Do you realize that those lists can make us enough money to really compete, to increase our advertising, to have more loss-leaders, to—here's something you probably didn't think about—to increase salaries, including yours? And what can be more right than helping these other salespeople sharpen their marketing lists? And what about our customers? They get a few more flyers in their mailboxes, maybe letting them know about a deal on something they want and need. And don't forget Molly Graubert. We sold her a list, and everybody was happy about that. She doubled her business, and no complaints."

"But the names we sell . . . . Those people—they don't . . . they didn't . . ."

"They didn't what? Didn't volunteer their names? Don't know about focus marketing? Come on, give them credit for something. Everybody sells lists, you know. Why do you think you get so much mail asking for donations to this and that charity? Because you gave once, that's why, and those people sold their list of donors to all the other charities. Nola, if charities can do it, why shouldn't private enterprise?"

"Yes, but . . ."

"No buts about it, Nola. Now, call those guys back and tell them we'll do it, or it's your job. I mean it. You made a mistake, and you've got to correct it."

In Hopedale, Massachusetts, Dick and Jane Jones relax in front of the TV, watching a travelogue all about Florida and its wonderful climate for retirees. Dick turns to Jane and says, "Now, that's my idea of retirement. We've talked about Florida. Do you think we should take a vacation there this year, to check it out for our retirement? It's only a couple of years away."

Jane is thrilled that he mentioned Florida. Why, just today in the mail she got a grand brochure on buying a Florida condominium. "Maybe we should try it out first, on a vacation, like you say. And maybe we should look into buying some housing while we're down there. We could look up those condos that Relaxed Retirement is advertising."

"Yeah. We sure can do better than staying here. You know, it's lucky we didn't get robbed like the Taylors next door, and those nine other working couples last week. In the middle of the day, too. Lucky you don't work. Why, it's almost as if those thieves had a list of old folks who have jobs to go to."

Case

3A

Role-Playing
Version

Something for Everyone

Recombination of Data at a Supermarket

Cast of Characters

Mary Smith, *homeowner, Happy Valley, MA*

John Smith, *Mary's husband*

Nola Brickell, *Information Systems Administrator for Chambord's Supermarket chain of 12 stores*

Pierre Nadeau, *General Manager of the Chambord chain, and Nola's immediate supervisor*

Mr. Crumphill, *head of marketing at Relaxed Retirement*

Mr. Campbell, *head of sales at Farwell Auto*

Dick Jones, *homeowner, Hopedale, MA*

Jane Jones, *Dick's wife*

Scene 1	The Smith residence on Elm Street, Happy Valley, Massachusetts. John is center stage, trimming a hedge. Mary is stage right at a mailbox, sorting the mail. She stops halfway, holding up a flyer.
Mary	[*turning toward John*] John, look! We got a coupon in the mail! It's a fifteen-dollar discount to have our dog Rover groomed. How did they know?
John	Know what?
Mary	Well, how did Molly's Pet Grooming Service know we have a dog? Do you suppose one of our neighbors told them about Rover?
John	Mary, I can't see how that's likely. It must be one of those hit-or-miss mass mailings. Anyway, let's use that coupon. It sure is a good deal.
Scene 2	*Chambord's Supermarket administrative offices, Griffin, Massachusetts.* Pierre's *desk is center stage.* Nola *sits at a desk stage left, with a desktop computer in front of her. The phone rings.* Nola *picks it up.*
Nola	Info Systems, Nola Griffin speaking. How may I help you?

Crumphill   I understand you're in charge there at Chambord's information systems. My name is Charles Crumphill. I'm in charge of marketing . . .

Nola   [*interrupting*] "Hold on a second—I'm putting you on the speaker phone. . . . OK, go.

[Pierre Nadeau *enters, sits at his desk, starts to work with papers.*]

Crumphill   I'm in charge of marketing at Relaxed Retirement. Perhaps you've heard of them. We handle all of the mail–order brochures for RR, and we want to try some focused marketing. Would you be interested in selling the names of selected Chambord customers? As Information Systems Manager, no doubt you can isolate the names and addresses of the people who buy old-age health stuff . . . you know, denture cream, corn plasters, and such.

Nola   Well, I'll have to check with my boss.

Crumphill   All right. But be sure to tell him there's money in it. We'll pay three dollars a name, with a fifty-dollar bonus for every sale.

[Pierre *stops his paperwork, obviously very interested in the phone conversation.*]

Nola   OK, get back to me tomorrow. 'Bye.

[Nola *hangs up, and the phone rings again.*]

Nola   Info Systems, Nola Griffin speaking. How may I help you?

Campbell   Nola? I'm head of auto sales at Farwell Auto, and you and I can help each other. I'm looking into a target marketing scheme . . . idea . . . where you'd give me the names of customers who bought maps, vacation planning guides, motor oil . . . you know, people who might need a new car. I'll pay Chambord's, of course, for every name, whether they buy or not. What do you think?

Nola   Well, I'll have to check with my boss.

Campbell   Do that. I know Pierre. I think he'll go for it.

[Pierre *signals* Nola *over to his desk.*]

Nola	OK, I've got to go now. Call tomorrow. 'Bye.
Nola	*[walking toward* Pierre's *desk]* What do you think of that? That's two more . . .
Pierre	What do you mean? We've had other calls?
Nola	Yeah. Just yesterday, a Mr. Cornwall, the floor manager from the appliance center at Brumble's Department Store, called. He wanted a list of the customers who . . . get this! . . . who didn't buy any frozen foods for two weeks in a row. He figured they wouldn't have a freezer. I told him no way, of course, just like I'll tell Crumphill and Campbell.
Pierre	Hey, Nola, you can't do that! Do you realize how much money there is in those lists? And it's free money, too. I mean, you can create those lists with no trouble at all, right? Am I right?
Nola	Yes, but . . . it's not right.
Pierre	Not right? What do you mean, not right?
Nola	"Well, it's not . . . we'd be making money on other people's names, and all."
Pierre	Hey, Nola, get off it. Our profit margin's so low, we feel good making forty cents on a bag of groceries, and you're telling me it's not right to improve our profit picture? Do you realize that those lists can make us enough money to really compete, to increase our advertising, to have more loss-leaders, to—here's something you probably didn't think about—to increase salaries, including yours? And what can be more right than helping these other salespeople sharpen their marketing lists? And what about our customers? They get a few more flyers in their mailboxes, maybe letting them know about a deal on something they want and need. And don't forget Molly Graubert. We sold her a list, and everybody was happy about that. She doubled her business, and no complaints.
Nola	But the names we sell . . . those people, they don't . . . they didn't . . .

Pierre	They didn't what? Didn't volunteer their names? Don't know about focus marketing? Come on, give them credit for something. Everybody sells lists, you know. Why do you think you get so much mail asking for donations to this and that charity? Because you gave once, that's why, and those people sold their list of donors to all the other charities. Hey, Nola, if charities can do it, why shouldn't private enterprise?
Nola	"Yes, but . . ."
Pierre	Hold on! What is it that's really bothering you?
Nola	I guess maybe it's the fact that we're making a profit at our customers' expense. I know, I know—that's our business. But here they don't have a choice about it. They don't even know about it. And even though a few might get some benefit out of it, what about all the others? It would be different if they knew, if they told us we could use their names, if we weren't using the data this way. . . .
Pierre	Hey, that's your job you're talking about, Nola. Now, call those guys back and tell them we'll do it. I mean it.
Scene 3	*The Jones residence on Main Street, Hopedale, Massachusetts.* Dick *and* Jane *relax in front of the TV, watching a travelogue.*
Dick	[*turning to Jane*] Now, that's my idea of retirement. We've talked about Florida. Do you think we should take a vacation there this year, to check it out for our retirement? It's only a couple of years away.
Jane	Why, just today in the mail we got a great brochure with details on how to buy a Florida condominium. Maybe we could try it out first, on a vacation, like you say. And maybe we could look into buying some housing while we're down there. We could look up those places that Relaxed Retirement is advertising.
Dick	Yeah. We sure can do better than staying here. You know, it's lucky we didn't get robbed like the Taylors next door, and those nine other working couples last week. In the middle of the day, too. Lucky you don't work. Why, it's almost as if those thieves had a list of old folks who have jobs to go to.

Case

4

Abort, Retry, Ignore

Recovery of Data Leads to Discovery of Confidential File

It was only 9:10 A.M. and Barry Larson had a problem. He was close to panic. His fingers darted over the keyboard again, repeating the DOS command. He kept hoping the system would just once be able to read the disk. "Just once," he thought, "and I'll back it up. Then I can print the report." But the luminous green message kept repeating

Directory error reading drive C: Abort, Retry, Ignore?

Barry was scheduled to attend the regular two-hour staff meeting in 20 minutes. And at 1:30 he was due to submit his quarterly projection report to William Burton, the comptroller of Cardamom Corporation. Barry was out of time. He snatched the phone from the cradle and dialed Technical Support. Barbara Dalton was at his desk in five minutes, with her all-time favorite file-recovery tool, Fixit.

"Did you try to write anything to the disk after you saw the message?"

"No! All I've done is try to get into my spreadsheet system!" Barry was almost shouting.

Barbara tried to reassure him. "No sweat, then. I should be able to recover all your files by the time you get back from your morning meeting."

Barry was relieved. He told Barbara, "The only file that's important to me is the worksheet called PROJECT3. Recover that one and the spreadsheet program, and I'll treat you to lunch for a week."

While Barry rushed off to his meeting, Barbara got to work. She started up Fixit in the floppy drive and identified drive C, the hard drive, as the corrupted target. Fixit's first listing showed many file names with a question mark for a prefix, including ?OMMAND, ?RINT, ?ORMAT. She also saw ?ROJECT3. When DOS "erases" a file, it only marks the file as erased by replacing the first character of the file name with a special character. Fixit simply displays that special character as a question mark. Barbara knew immediately what Barry had done. He had intended to erase the files from a diskette in his floppy drive; instead, by accident, he had addressed his C drive and erased the files there.

"This should be a snap," she thought. "?OMMAND is COMMAND. ?RINT is PRINT. . . ."

She started the repairs. System files were easy, as were the spreadsheet files, which all ended with the extension .WKS. She also saw ?ROJECT3 and immediately changed that to PROJECT3. In 10 minutes she had done all that Barry had asked for. However, Barbara felt that she should rescue more files because she had the time. She continued her cleanup of the disk.

The other data files—worksheets and word processing text files—were harder. Barry had made up the names of these files according to some association scheme tied to the contents of the file. First Barbara renamed the files that were preceded with question marks, changing each ? to an X. ?OSB became XOSB and ?TOCREP became XTOCREP.

At this point, Barbara could have left the system for Barry to rename all files as he intended. Barbara, though, was a perfectionist. In only 20 minutes Barbara had recovered the contents of the hard disk, but she knew that the disk directory still needed touching up. Barry would have to rename all X-prefixed files to their original names. Barbara knew that Barry would be pressed for time, so she decided to help him out. She was pretty sure that a glance at a file's contents would be sufficient to figure out the file name. She brought up the word processor and started scanning the files, renaming them as she went. XOSB was a memo to the Bank of South Boston, so she changed the file name to BOSB. XTOCREP was a stock report. She changed it to STOCREP.

After cleaning up the text files, Barbara got into the spreadsheet system to look at those files. The first one, XERSON, came as a complete surprise. It was a listing of Cardamom's personnel, including their current annual salaries, promotion histories, medical leaves, garnishments, disciplinary actions, potential promotions, and personal family data. She thought, "Barry does a great job as a financial analyst for Mr. Burton, but what in the world is he doing with confidential personnel information?"

She immediately renamed the file PERSON, trying hard not to look at the contents. Then she continued through the rest of the files, scanning their content just enough to rename the files appropriately. After verifying that there were no more files with the X or the ? prefix on the disk, she tested the system. It worked well, and she felt confident that Barry could reclaim and print his critical quarterly project file. As Barbara returned to her office, she was still wondering about the confidential file.

Case

5

Messages from All Over

Who Controls the Content of E-Mail and BBS?

The HMV Corporation is one of the largest designers and manufacturers of distributed computer systems. Its phenomenal growth in the last decade is due in large measure to its attention to networking technology. It makes extensive use of its own product, operating one of the largest computer networks in the world. Most of HMV's 107,000 employees have access to the network, and they are encouraged to use it. The two most popular network services the HMV employees enjoy are their own bulletin board system, or BBS, and e-mail.

The BBS is intended to serve exactly as the name implies, as a sort of computer-managed announcement board. The company encourages its employees to swap technical information openly and quickly. A user interested in new developments in supercooled switches would have to enter only a few descriptive words, such as "cryogenic & switching time & superconductive," to get all messages relating to the topic. HMV's policy allows the BBS users to treat the board as a kind of classified-ads network. Although the majority of messages are of the "Notice" variety, an increasing number of "Wanted" and "For Sale" items appear. An employee interested in buying a house from a fellow HMV worker might enter, for example, "3BR & house & Chicago."

The e-mail system is intended as the private communications medium for the company. The user may send messages to one or many receivers. Messages to groups of users, such as those in regional offices or specific research labs, are about as common as messages from one individual to another. Of course, if someone wanted to send a message to all HMV employees, that user would use the BBS.

Horace Ganglion is the Network Administrator. His responsibilities, aside from keeping the system running at all times, include on-line monitoring of BBS message content. He must keep the BBS from becoming too cluttered with items that would more properly belong in a newspaper. Also, he must ensure appropriate use of the e-mail system.

Bill is Horace's Assistant Network Administrator. He has asked to see Horace on a matter of some urgency. Bill's responsibilities include acting as liaison between network users and Horace. Bill shows Horace a hard-copy listing of messages he selected while scanning the traffic out of curiosity. Horace sees that this list is a photocopied compilation of selected messages. The first group of messages were all on the BBS:

Notice: Some PC clones (Shrinq, Dill, Howland-Parker, others) bomb when moving data from one open file to another when using MegaWrite. For more info contact . . .
Voters: Send Washington a message! Dump the Pres and vote for Reform!

For Sale: Indonesian love slave. Grants your every wish, Contact . . .
Notice: Are there any real sports out there ready for a fun indoor game?
Contact . . .
Wanted: Decent word processor, manuals unnecessary, no questions asked.
Contact . . .

The second group were e-mail messages that Bill had selected:

To: Jim Schiffer, VP Mktg
From: Joan Hicks, Phoenix Training Center Stock Manager
Subject: Available Hardware

Our office has several used PC clones available for internal sale at a very reasonable price. Those not sold internally will be greatly discounted on the open
market. Send me a message if you're interested.

To: Margo Lasker, Manager, Systems Development Group
From: Lizbeth Winston
Subject: Dorothy Vinson

Among many other comments I have received concerning Dorothy's work
performance are the following: "Incapable of approaching business negotiations in a professional, rational, and mature manner . . .," ". . . shouldn't be
trusted . . .," "her actions were intended to alarm, manipulate, antagonize, or
further disrupt the process . . ."

What do you suggest I do now?

To: Mary Trask
From: Bill, your good friend
Subject: Private consultation

Are you interested in some indoor sport?

To: Roger Delacroix
From: Armand Martin
Subject: Termination

One more leak about that Garfinkel deal behind my back, and you're gone,
buster! I'm the boss around here, and if I say Garfinkel is clean and knows what
he's doing, then that's the way it is. I don't care what kind of dirt you might
have dug up on him—he stays our contractor. And the fact that he's my cousin
has nothing to do with it. Got it?

Bill asks Horace, "What are you going to do about this?"

Case

6

A Job on the Side

An Employee Is Tempted to Consult Part-Time

Mitron is a billion-dollar computer hardware and software vendor. Anthony Frasier is a software-support analyst for Mitron's midwest field office. Anthony is on the phone with customers much of the time. He reports the customers' program bugs to Engineering, and he gives his customers software patches or workarounds directly over the phone lines, computer-to-computer, whenever possible.

When Anthony hears about especially difficult software problems, he takes his expertise to the customer personally. Until last year, his on-site support and occasional user training were provided as a part of the customers' maintenance contracts. That practice became so popular that it was too expensive for Mitron. They had to change the policy of free support and training, so they unbundled the support services from the maintenance contract. Now Mitron charges its customers separately for on-site support services.

Mitron suffered during the past recession. Management's response to the crunch was to freeze all salaries for 18 months. Twelve months have passed, and Mitron still hurts. Some people have been laid off, and Anthony suspects that his days are numbered. However, he knows he is still valuable to Mitron; his supervisor told him that he'd be the first to get a raise, if that were possible.

One of Mitron's largest customers and one of Anthony's most important clients is the state government. Over the years, he has established a close relationship with many key state employees. The state has several sites where employees need a lot of technical help and training. The users prefer to contract with Mitron rather than to develop the expertise from within. Anthony has been working closely with Mary Coulter in the State Information Systems Office. They know each other well and have developed an enviable level of mutual trust.

Yesterday, Mary called Anthony. "Anthony, I have a proposition for you to think about. I think you'll like it."

"Tell me. I'm especially ready for good news."

"State needs someone at the Pastoria site to help out with their new system. It's the new PAX 3355 system your people installed this summer, and they need support and training in the worst way. It's right up your alley. Want to do it?"

"Sure. Send up the paperwork and I'll get started."

"Wait, you don't understand. I want *you* to do this, not Mitron. If we have to get you through your company, it'll take months of paperwork. And we have to pay the Mitron overhead fees, besides."

"Gee, I don't know, Mary. You're asking me to do something on my own that my company pays me for. Isn't that a conflict of interest?"

"Well, that depends. Your company's present policy on that really should change, don't you think? The rules on employees taking on a second job are so much more strict at Mitron than with your competitors, for example. Policies do change based on demand, after all. Remember, you guys unbundled service from maintenance. Anyhow, we want you rather than some other consultant we don't know, even if they're cheaper. You know, success at this site in Pastoria means a lot of future business to Mitron. My feeling is that they'd go along with this if we explained it to your management."

"Why don't you? What's the rush? Why don't you present your case to our management? Maybe they can hurry up the process, get you an answer in a couple of weeks."

"Anthony, you don't understand. We can't wait that long. And the sooner the system is up and running, the better it will be for the entire state. Don't forget that one of the big reasons we got this system was to reduce the delay of payment on welfare and unemployment compensation. We won't ask you for any time that would interfere with your normal work schedule. You name the hours, show up when you can, and we know you'll do the job. To make it worth your while, we'll pay you 20 percent above the usual consulting fee, and give you a $10,000 bonus when you're through. That's how much we would have to pay Mitron when we include its administrative overhead."

Anthony said nothing. He is pleased that his reputation is so good. He is overwhelmed at the generosity of the offer. He considers it to be the chance to start up a decent nest egg in case he's laid off. He wonders at the consequences if word gets out . . .

The New Job

An Offensive Graphic Image Appears in an Office Environment

Iris Blair is really upset, and she seems to have no one to go to. Two weeks ago, she was brimming with excitement about her new job. Now, she wonders whether she should quit.

Tolliver Investments is a rising star in the highly competitive field of brokerage houses. It's only three years old, and it has grown from a trio of entrepreneurs with a few loyal friends as its customers to a company with 37 employees and lots of hustle. Tolliver has succeeded in a tight economy where many others have failed, in large measure because of the 15 brokers that make up the Customer Service Group.

Iris has been with Tolliver Investments for two weeks. In her newly created job of Applications Manager, Iris installs, maintains, and upgrades all the company's software tools, from word processors, spreadsheet programs, and utilities, to graphics and statistical packages. She and Terry Sullivan, the Customer Services Manager, report directly to Roy Tolliver, the president and CEO. Iris knows that her performance for the next several weeks will be the deciding factor in her career.

Tolliver's Customer Services Group is the backbone of the company. The brokers have available to them all the modern technology possible in each of their offices. Each office has a 12-line phone system, a color scanner, a color laser printer, and three high-resolution color graphics computers, each one capable of accessing, as a terminal, any stock market worldwide. The terminal users also access the Internet as necessary. The computers also can act as independent workstations to perform financial analyses, word processing, or any other standalone activity.

Terry Sullivan's idea of management is that it's best to have the brokers in the offices slightly out of control and free to think for themselves, so his grip on them is loose, almost detached. Terry knows that those 15 people are the company's breadwinners and that each earns about as much on commission as Roy Tolliver does. They could leave anytime, so they have to be kept happy.

Two nights ago, after most people had left, Iris was in the office of Arthur Amanita and Ronald Conway, two of the most highly respected brokers at Tolliver. Her job was to install a new virus-protection program. She noticed that Art and Ron's optical disks were in their protective cases, properly shelved away from the hardware. Art and Ron were gone for the day, but they had left her a note that they were having trouble printing some graphics they had downloaded from an Internet site. Iris first installed the virus-protection software, then proceeded to work on the graphics printing problem. She loaded the file, changed the file's extension so that the printer's software could recognize it as a color graphic, and issued the PRINT command. The printer started normally and scrolled its graphic image. It showed a bikini-clad woman in a provocative pose. Iris shut down Art's computer, and repeated the process on Ron's computer. The printer displayed exactly the same graphic image as Art's.

Yesterday morning, Iris was in early, as usual. When she saw Art and Ron go past her office, she approached them and told them that she had installed the virus-protection software last night.

Art said, "So, what do you think of our downloaded graphics?"

Iris replied, "Why don't you guys grow up? That's so childish."

Art's smile disappeared. He faced Iris and said nothing, his eyes burning into hers. Then he grinned. "Iris, you need to loosen up. Tell you what. How about you and me stopping by Googol's Bar after work. Then I'll treat you to dinner, and who knows what after?"

"Thanks, but no. I expect I'll still be here tonight when you're long gone."

"Fine by me," Art said. But obviously it was not.

At noon today, Iris passed by Art's office. Art wasn't in, but Ron was in his next-door office. He called her to his desk. "Wait a second. You want to see our latest Internet printout? It's a major improvement."

He issued the PRINT command, and this time the color printer showed a woman in full-frontal nudity.

Iris fumed. "That's really tasteless and insensitive. You should know better." She heard Ron's reply behind her as she stomped out of the office.

"Hey, it's your fault. Maybe you shouldn't have refused Art's invitation."

Iris sees Roy Tolliver and Art laughing together at the coffee counter. She knows it's about the start-up screen. She catches Tolliver glancing in her direction and lowering his voice. They laugh again, this time more quietly. It's obvious to Iris that these two are doing their male bonding at her expense. "That's just great," she thinks. "Now there's no telling what I might find the next time I help out those guys. It's got me thinking. Maybe it's time to blow the whistle on this situation."

Case

7A

Role-Playing
Version

The New Job

An Offensive Graphic Image Appears in an Office Environment

Cast of Characters

Sally Burdette, *Iris's good friend and Tolliver receptionist*
Iris Blair, *newly appointed Applications Manager*
Terry Sullivan, *Customer Services Manager*
Arthur Amanita, *broker*
Ronald Conway, *broker*

Scene 1	*The Upper Crust sandwich shop.* Sally *and* Iris *sit across from each other at a small table. This is* Iris's *first day working for Tolliver Investments, and she is anxious to share her excitement with* Sally, *who is her best friend and coincidentally the receptionist at Tolliver.*
Sallly	So tell me all about it. What do you think of your new job?
Iris	It sure is different. It's a big challenge and a big responsibility.
Sally	I heard. You manage the Group's programs.
Iris	Those guys are phenomenal! I had no idea that the Customer Services Group was so important, even after Mr. Tolliver said those fifteen guys were the backbone of the company.
Sally	Call him Roy.
Iris	Huh?
Sally	Mr. Tolliver. Call him Roy. He really likes it. It makes him feel more a part of the group. [*Pause.*] Yeah, I know what you mean. Just look at all the equipment they have: a twelve-line phone in each office, those high-resolution color graphics computers, the color scanners, color printers, all with access through the network to the Internet, and to Mother, their big computer, the . . . you know . . .
Iris	Yeah, the central server. Say, Sally, don't you think it's weird, in a way? You know, fifteen guys, macho as all get-out, all tapping into a central computer they call Mother?

Sally	That's the way they like it, and that's the way Terry likes to manage the group. Has Terry briefed you yet?
Iris	No, but thanks for mentioning it. I have to leave right now to see him.
Scene 2	Terry Sullivan's *office.* Terry *sits at his desk, surrounded by his three computers.* Iris *walks in, and* Terry *rises to offer her a seat in the only other chair in his office.*
Terry	Iris, it's good having you aboard. Have a seat. Make yourself comfortable. This won't take long. I just want to check with you, see if you have any questions.
Iris	[*sitting in the offered chair*] Thanks. Wow! This outfit is even more impressive than what I imagined after seeing it the first time, you know, when you and . . . uh, Roy . . . and I talked a week ago.
Terry	It isn't too much for you, is it? I mean, we hired you as an upper-level manager because of your great credentials. Are you getting familiar with our software tools?
Iris	Yes, no problem with the usual—the word processors, spreadsheets, utilities—and I'm getting the hang of the graphics and stat packages. I don't think there'll be any problem there either.
Terry	That's good to hear. Now, let me remind you how I like to manage the guys. Those fifteen men are the company's money makers. Each earns about as much as Roy does, when you count their commission. They could leave anytime, so my job is mainly keeping them happy. I do that by getting them the latest equipment and staying out of their way. They like to be slightly out of control and free to think for themselves, so my grip on them is really loose. We're a team, in a way. Your job as applications manager keeps them in the top-of-the-line software, and mine is to satisfy their independent egos with the hardware.
Iris	You make it sound like they're a bunch of independent egotists in love with their hardware.
Terry	That's not too far off. They're the ones in the front lines.

Iris	Sure, but it's only coincidental, isn't it, that there isn't a single female in the group? I mean, you . . . Tolliver Investments . . . have tried to get women as brokers?
Terry	Oh, of course. Last year we had two women, but they didn't last. They just didn't fit in, I guess. They both quit after a few weeks, no reason given, and went to work for another investment firm. Made out OK, too, so I hear.
Scene 3	*Two weeks later, at the Upper Crust sandwich shop.*
Sally	So, tell me. You wanted to talk. Trouble with Terry?
Iris	Yeah, maybe . . . I don't know. . . . Something's bothering me. I have to talk to somebody about it.
Sally	It's not Terry, is it? You and he are chummy. I see you in his office often.
Iris	That's different. We talk about the job . . . you know . . . the hardware and software. This has nothing to do with that. It's about Art and Ron, and their graphics downloads from the Internet.
Sally	Huh? What's that?
Iris	Well, all the brokers have color printers and color scanners and access to the Internet. So they surf the Internet—that's what it's called when you look around for interesting files—and they get color graphics files to copy from the net to their hardware.
Sally	Sure. That's one of the reasons they're so happy here. Terry gives them just about anything they want. Pretty much lets them do anything they want with that hardware, too.
Iris	I understand that. It's Terry's style of management. But let me finish. Last night, I was working late. I had to install a new anti-virus program in all the brokers' workstations. I went from one office to another, booting each system, and when I got to Art's computer, I saw that he'd left me a note. It said that he and Ron were having some trouble printing a graphic file they'd downloaded from the Internet. I printed it out and it was a woman in a bikini, and she was, well, she was . . . let's say highly exposed.

Sally	So? Hey, it's his printer, his machine. If he has to remind himself what a woman looks like, so be it.
Iris	But he knew that I was going to install an anti-virus update. And Art wasn't the only one. Ron's graphic was exactly the same picture.
Sally	Well, I wouldn't let it bother you. If you ignore it, maybe they'll tone it down after a while. You know, those two are the top guys as far as the brokers go. They're Roy's good friends. You don't want to cross them.
Scene 4	Iris *is in her office.* Art *goes past her door.*
Iris	[*rising*] Art . . . Got a minute?
Art	Sure. What's up?"
Iris	Just thought I'd let you know I installed that new virus-protection software last night.
Art	So, what do you think of my color graphic?
Iris	I saw it, and Ron's too. Why don't you guys grow up? That's so childish.

[Art's *smile disappears. He faces* Iris *and says nothing. His eyes are hard. Then he smiles.*]

Art	Iris, you need to loosen up. Get a life. Tell you what. How about you and me stopping by Googol's Bar after work? Then I'll treat you to dinner, and who knows what after?
Iris	Thanks, but no thanks. I expect I'll still be here tonight when you're long gone.
Art	[*obviously angry*] Fine by me.
Scene 5	*One day later.* Iris *passes by* Ron's *office. His door is open. He sees her.*
Ron	Iris! Wait a second. Do you want to see our latest graphic? It's a major improvement.
Iris	Sure, as long as it's not that silly pin-up.

[Ron *displays a new picture and stands back to show* Iris.]

Ron

There! Now isn't that better? Art and I call it FFN for Full Frontal Nudity!

Iris

[*fuming*] That's really tasteless and insensitive. You should know better.

[Iris *stomps out.*]

Ron

[*shouting*] Hey, it's your fault. Maybe you shouldn't have refused Art's invitation.

Scene 6

The Upper Crust sandwich shop.

Sally

Gee, Iris, you look down in the dumps. More trouble with Art and Ron?

Iris

Yeah. Bad. You heard about their new downloaded color graphics. If that wasn't bad enough, this morning I saw Roy and Art laughing together at the coffee counter. Roy saw me looking and he immediately lowered his voice. Then he and Art laughed again, more quietly. What gets me, Sally, is they were doing their male bonding at my expense! Now there's no telling what I might find the next time I boot a system. It's got me thinking. Maybe it's time to blow the whistle on this situation.

The Buyout

Inappropriately Acquired Data Prompts Personnel Problems

Agaric Software started small, grew fast, and met its fate in a quick buyout by Spectran Corporation. At first, Agaric employees assumed they would keep their autonomy and operate with little change in management or method. Such was not to be the case. Spectran wanted a merger so that Agaric would be a branch office, with only a portion of its original staff.

Mary Marver has been General Manager of Agaric for three years. Her staff respects and admires her for her managerial ability and her loyalty. They call her Marverlous Mary. She knows about the nickname and likes it.

Mary has participated in all negotiations with Spectran, so she is aware of the eventual fate of some of its employees. Filed under the name PROJTEN, she has a Lotus spreadsheet that projects future employment of the staff. It lists present workers, their current projects, their lengths of tenure at Agaric, their current salaries, and their scheduled termination dates. Mary protects this file with an encryption utility called DESCANT. This program uses the Data Encryption Standard (DES) algorithm to jumble any file via a key, or password, supplied by the user. Mary's password is MARVERLOUS.

Louis Shuster, an employee at Agaric, answers his phone. "Hello. Louis Schuster here."

"Hi, Lou. Rick. Hey, it looks like we Pattersons will get to live in the country. Sally and I found the house we want. It's a beaut. Can't wait to tell you about it. How about lunch at noon?"

"Sure. See you in the cafeteria. Bye."

Louis Shuster and Rick Patterson have been with Agaric for years. They are tight and trusting friends. Rick is, at this moment, critically important to the company's future success with Spectran. He is managing the transfer of all service accounts from Agaric to Spectran's support staff. His value is due in large measure to his upbeat outlook and friendly attitude with outsiders. Louis's job is entirely different. He deals with Agaric programmers only, and then just to get bugs fixed or to get upgrades to the software he uses.

Unknown to Louis and Rick, they are both included in Spectran's decision to reduce the payroll by 25 percent. Spectran wanted this cut to occur on May 1, with no notice but with a two-week-salary severance package. Mary Marver had argued with Spectran: She said the people must be kept until the transfer of all Agaric customers was complete. Spectran agreed to hold off the cuts until June 1, the deadline for transfer, but not any longer. They also agreed, at Mary's insistence, that all people to be terminated would be given a minimum of one month's notice to reduce their personal hardships. But Spectran's management insists that Rick is an exception. He must not be told of his impending layoff until the end of the contract, because he must keep a "happy face" during his work with the clients. Spectran's explanation was simple: "Rick Patterson is valuable to us until June 1. After that date, his job will be assumed by people in Spectran. It would be counterproductive to keep him on the payroll for a month if his job is gone."

On May 1, all affected employees, except Rick, are notified of the massive layoff a month away. Louis is one of the notified workers, and he is understandably upset, but only for a few days. He quickly finds another job, and he will start work for his new company in two weeks. Louis is glad that Rick was not one of those given notice.

While still working at Agaric, Louis needs the name of a project proposal. He knows that the names, both tentative and final, are in a file on Mary's hard disk. He must find the name to complete his work, so he looks for Mary to ask her for a copy of the name file. Mary is tied up in meetings, so Louis sits at her desktop computer and boots it. Mary's directory lists a file called PROJTEN, but he sees it's been protected by DESCANT. He assumes the name PROJTEN stands for PROJect TENtative. He has no idea what Mary's password is. He looks around. Nothing is taped to her desk or the computer, no strange name is penciled onto the desk edge, there is no family picture with kids' names. He thinks a minute. "What would Marverlous Mary use ? . . . That's it!"

Louis types MARVERLOUS as a password and gains access to PROJTEN. It's a worksheet. He brings it up onto the screen and sees some names and projects, but one glance tells him that none of the listed projects is tentative. Then he notices the column headings "Tenure at Agaric" and "Termination date." He sees his own name with the date June 1. Rick Patterson is there too, with the same date. But Rick wasn't notified. Has some mistake been made?

Louis restores the computer to its original state and returns to his desk to finish the day. He is reluctant to say anything because he has invaded Mary's private file. The next three days are agony to Louis, but he keeps quiet.

On the fourth day after Louis saw Mary's file, his phone rings. He thinks, "I bet that's Rick. They finally told him." He picks up the phone. "Hello, Louis Shuster here."

"Hi, Lou. Rick. Guess what?"

"Yeah, I know. Isn't it awful? I thought about telling you, but . . ."

"Awful? What do you mean, Lou? It's great! Sally just called. She borrowed on our insurance and made the down payment on that house. Just had to call you to let you know. Looks like my luck is holding. Now what did you what to tell me?"

"Well, er . . . Rick, let me think about it. I'll call you later."

Charades

A Stolen Password and Its After-Effects

"Good morning, class. This week's assignment is simple. See if you can get into the school's mainframe operating system. You've been reading all about password protection and its weaknesses. Now you're to see if you can beat the RACS Network. If you succeed in stealing a network user's password, you are to log in to his or her account, print a simple document with the user name on top, as usual, and log off. You are not to add, delete, or modify any of the user's files. Otherwise, there are no rules. Anything goes, even social engineering. To the limit, people."

Dr. Peter Proctor's class, called Computer Security and Privacy, is one of Lagonda College's most popular, due in large part to Dr. Proctor's challenging "TTL" assignments. His students call them TTLs because he generally uses the phrase "to the limit" for emphasis.

Last week, Dr. Proctor demonstrated social engineering. Social engineering is a confidence game that hackers use on unwary timesharing users to steal their passwords. It involves the use of intimidation, pretense, gall, and outright lying. He called a fellow faculty member and said, "Sorry to interrupt your busy schedule. This is Karl Oberfest, systems administrator. I need your password to check your account for a possible virus. Afterwards you can change it. . . . OK, thanks."

Florence Porter and Ann Galen are two of the top students in the class. They generally plot together to solve the TTLs. This time, though, Florence decides to go it alone. They are sitting side by side at two terminals in the student computer lab.

"Ann, I just can't seem to get logged in. I've tried and tried, but I get bounced off every time. I bet there's something wrong with this terminal."

"Oh, come on! You know better than that. It's got to be something you're doing wrong in your log-in procedure. Try again, only slower."

Florence bashes the keys once more. Again, she turns to Ann. "I just can't get it. Ann, I know it sounds silly, but just log off and switch terminals with me and *you* try it. Please."

Ann and Florence switch places. Ann sees this on the screen:

RACS Network
USER NAME:>

Ann enters her user name, "Galen." The screen now shows:

USER NAME:>Galen
PASSWORD:

Ann looks around. Florence has turned her back, a common courtesy to avoid discovering another's password. Ann enters her password carefully, one character at a time, and receives this message:

Access denied on try 1.
Disconnected. Reconnect to try again.

"Curious," she thinks. She knows she has two more tries after reconnecting. She tries again.

RACS Network
USER NAME:>Galen
PASSWORD:>********
Welcome to RACS Operating System
$

"Florence! I got in. It was just a fluke."

"Yes, Florence? You got someone's password without their knowledge? Let's see your printout." Dr. Proctor is clearly surprised and pleased. The printout shows Ann Galen's name at the top. "Ann, were you aware that your password was compromised? You didn't give it to Florence, did you?"
"Of course not! But how did she do it? I'm very careful about that."
Florence explains. "I wrote a program that displays the system's prompts. Then I pretended that I had trouble logging in, remember? We switched terminals and you thought you were logging in. But you were really interacting with my program, not the system. It captured your password and placed it in a file in my account, then gave you the 'Disconnected' message and logged off. When you logged in a second time, you weren't in my account anymore, but in the system. It's called the charade technique. Clever, huh?"
Dr. Proctor reminded the class about the hazards of social engineering and congratulated Florence for a job well done. He further explained the charade technique and several other common methods for stealing passwords.

Case

10

Laccaria and Eagle

Restrictive Trade Practices Call for Hard Purchasing Decisions

Laccaria is a large third-world country. Its new military government understands the strategic importance of a strong information technology industry. Government officials feel that, to encourage technological growth, they must impose strict protectionist measures. These will help ensure that emerging Laccarian firms will be able to take full advantage of the domestic market, the ninth largest in the world. The trade barriers and high tariffs are not imposed on larger-scale computers, arbitrarily classified as mainframes by Laccarian officials.

The imposition of these protectionist measures has resulted in the formation of many small and medium-sized high-tech firms. They either assemble components imported from abroad or manufacture Laccarian clones of equipment made by large U.S. vendors such as Epsilon. In many cases, the locally produced equipment is copied exactly from U.S. equipment—often without licensing agreements.

Many software houses in Laccaria support this manufacturing effort. Although the government of Laccaria has international copyright agreements with the United States, Laccarian officials often look the other way, allowing local software houses to make and market unauthorized copies of U.S. software.

Multinational corporations operating branches or subsidiaries in Laccaria have felt the effect of the protectionist measures. It is difficult to get the right hardware configurations to run the software specifically designed for use at overseas sites. Sometimes, a planned system cannot be implemented because some critical part, such as a modem, is not available in Laccaria.

Eagle Bank is a large holding company headquartered in the United States. Its network of international offices covers nearly 40 countries. At most of these international sites, Eagle Bank has installed the Epsilon System 45 from Epsilon Corporation of Syracuse, New York. The hardware uses Eagle's Corporate Core Software Package. However, all seven of the Eagle-Laccaria sites are operating in batch mode with punched cards and tape drives. The systems haven't been upgraded because the Laccarian government's Informatics Bureau lists the System 45 as a minicomputer, so it cannot be imported from the United States or neighboring countries.

The manager of Eagle-Laccaria's head office asked Carlo, his IS manager, to contact Orista, the Laccarian vendor that makes a system similar to the System 45. The Laccarian system is called the Orista 45K. Carlo discovered that using these clones would force major changes to the Corporate Core Software Package, and that the hardware price was $270,000—more than twice the price of the same configuration in the United States. Carlo also found that the Orista 45K hardware was unreliable and subject to frequent breakdowns, that Orista lacked what he called "a properly trained maintenance staff," and that the firm offered poor support.

Carlo's next step was to talk to his contact at the Informatics Bureau. When Carlo asked what could be done, his bureau contact suggested that Eagle-Laccaria purchase an Epsilon mainframe, the 4311, a machine manufactured by Epsilon in Laccaria. Unfortunately, it costs $380,000—$30,000 higher than its U.S. price.

During the discussion, Colonel Cuervo of the Informatics Bureau warned Carlo not to get into difficulty by purchasing a "parallel market" System 45. These are Epsilon System 45s that have been brought into the country illegally. These may look tempting, he said, because they cost only $120,000 and are made in the United States. However, these "unofficial import channels" are not recognized by the government, which considers them detrimental to the economy of Laccaria. Carlo knows, though, that many firms in Laccaria, some competing directly with Eagle, have these illegal machines. The government rarely prosecutes violators of its protectionist policy.

The manager must make his decision. Carlo has supplied him with this simple summary table:

MACHINE	SOURCE	COST	NOTES
Orista 45K	Orista	$270,000	Unreliable
			Poor service
			Software changes necessary
			Good for local economy, based on the government's economic policy
Epsilon 4311	Epsilon-Laccaria	$380,000	Too much machine
			Software conversions needed
Epsilon 45	Parallel market	$120,000	No changes to software
			Known entity
			Bad for local economy, based on the government's economic policy

The manager studies the table and tells Carlo, "It's obvious, isn't it?"

Is it?

Case

11

Taking Bad with Good

The Software Is Bad, So Don't Pay for It

Aldrich & Royce (A&R) is a multimillion-dollar financial services company that used old batch-oriented programs for its daily operations. As a result, it became less competitive. It was desperate to replace the batch system with an up-to-date networked system of applications. The Information Systems department targeted two batch programs for immediate replacement. One performed stock-and-bond analysis, and the other managed client transactions.

MegaMerge Software is the developer of MoneyMaker, a financial-analysis applications package sold to small investment firms. Among its several subprograms, two were of special interest to the Information Systems department of A&R. FINSTAT performs analyses on stocks and bonds, and CLIENTS manages buyer transactions. MegaMerge has never tried MoneyMaker at any site larger than Murdock's, the local investment company, which has a multiuser microcomputer with eight terminals in separate offices. Murdock's was considered to be MegaMerge's beta test site. That is, MegaMerge gave Murdock's the package of applications free of charge, with the understanding that Murdock's would report any bugs to MegaMerge.

A number of key people from A&R's Information Systems (IS) department observed MoneyMaker in operation at Murdock's and saw that it was an excellent tool. They liked FINSTAT especially. The department decided to purchase MoneyMaker, aware that it would have to customize the programs to suit its own unique needs. The contract specified that A&R purchase MoneyMaker for $25,000 payable upon delivery, plus $1,200 a month for maintenance and upgrades.

The company invested time and money to assemble a conversion team. This so-called Project X Team was a group of 14 new employees, some permanent and some contract workers. The Project X Team's objective was to change MoneyMaker from a client system for a small, single-site investment office to one that would work in a much larger network environment.

A&R knew that MoneyMaker had not been fully tested, so it included these points in its contract with MegaMerge:

- Buyer (Aldrich & Royce) is aware of the "raw" nature of the product.

- Seller (MegaMerge) will supply buyer with four new releases per year to add new functionality to the system and to correct minimal bugs.

- Seller makes no guarantee of safety or accuracy of the package.

- Seller is responsible for "functional generic package errors." If such errors occur, Seller will fix them and give Buyer the code or create a new release.

The contract did *not* include:

■   A standard for testing the software.

■   A statement of the amount of testing Seller would do before the package was released.

■   A disclaimer clause proclaiming Seller not responsible for Buyer's lost profits or damage to Buyer's reputation due to problems with software.

From the first day of testing by Project X programmers, it became evident that MoneyMaker had both very good and very bad features. The stock-and-bond analysis program, FINSTAT, was far better than anything A&R had used in the past—even better than MegaMerge's sales representative had said it was. Also in FINSTAT's favor, it worked beautifully in A&R's networked environment, equally well at all sites.

Unfortunately, the other MoneyMaker program, CLIENTS, which A&R wanted to use to replace its client-management program, was a total disaster. It worked fine in a small environment, but no amount of rewriting could make it operate efficiently and accurately in a large network.

A&R had spent much time and money in its efforts to customize MoneyMaker, but it could only make use of FINSTAT. Besides the conversion costs, A&R had paid MegaMerge $9,600 for maintenance for eight months. The firm had received quarterly upgrades from MegaMerge, but none helped the problems with CLIENT. The IS department's manager estimated that, without CLIENT in operation, 50 percent of MoneyMaker's functionality was gone.

After consulting with the IS department manager, the Chief Financial Officer of A&R decided to reduce the maintenance and upgrade fee of $1,200 to $600 a month in compensation for the lost value of CLIENT.

When MegaMerge's manager heard of this reduction in payments and the reasons for it, he had his best programmer write a virus program to destroy all MegaMerge programs at A&R. The virus was placed in the next upgrade shipment to A&R. When A&R installed that upgrade, the virus destroyed all MegaMerge programs, including FINSTAT, which had become A&R's workhorse program.

<table>
<tr><td>Case</td></tr>
</table>

12

The Engineer and the Teacher

Copyright Ethics in Schools and Industry

My name is Harrison Grander. Three months ago, I was hired as Senior Engineer by Googalong Consultants in Dallas. The firm's clients are local utility companies that need solutions to civil, structural, mechanical, and electrical problems. I manage these projects and deal with the associated clients.

The competition for winning consulting contracts is fierce. When my company started in business two years ago, it had only a few personal computers and the bare minimum of engineering, accounting, and office automation software. As the company grew, it added more PCs and circulated more copies of the original software, along with unauthorized versions of more sophisticated software tools. There were no funds to buy legitimate software. In fact, the company canceled maintenance contracts on the hardware and operating system software during these lean times.

Now, we're located in a new office park. Business is booming in a slumping economy, because the company focus is on quality work at a reasonable price. Just yesterday my boss told me that he wanted me to take over as manager of Information Systems Resources. It's not that big a deal. It takes only one day a week to keep track of all the software we have, making sure we have backups of the most recent versions and so on.

What bothers me is what I found on the job during the first day. The company's most important software, the engineering package we use all the time, the one that is the envy of all our competition, was never purchased. It is a bootlegged copy.

Well, of course I went to my boss.

He said, "My gosh! You don't expect us to buy that now, do you? The least expensive version is $10,000. Spending that kind of money would set us back years against the competition. I expect we'll be able to afford it in a year or two, but right now we wouldn't be able to make competitive bids if we were to buy it."

My name is Esther Gooch. Three months ago, I was employed as an adult education teacher for a consortium of several San Francisco-area schools. This group of schools has set a goal for me and the other AE teachers: We must teach relevant skills and technologies to the area's adult population. Unfortunately, the recent budget cuts undertaken in California towns and cities have forced the teaching staff to stretch all existing resources. We are asked to teach computing without having adequate software.

When I first began three months ago, I was told by my fellow teachers that the only way we could make an impact would be to teach the skills that sell, such as word processing and spreadsheet development, and to use the most current and popular software. Of course, I agreed. But I pointed out that site licenses for these products are expensive and we are under budget constraints. I told them that a viable alternative is single-copy versions of decent, though less popular, software packages that are often available, free, as freeware.

My fellow teachers disagreed with using freeware. They argued that we have a moral right—and maybe even an obligation—to make multiple copies of "good" software to distribute to as many educators as might find it useful, whether or not we have the licenses. Even the administrators turn their heads at the practice. They feel the same way the teachers do: Without copied software, the students would not learn the leading-edge software and would stop coming to our classes. Ultimately, we'd be out of a job.

On the other hand, I have a hard time swallowing the software developers' claim that our copying causes them to lose money on potential sales to schools. There's no way we could buy it. Besides, by exposing our students to the software, we're training a large pool of potential future customers. I think it's my moral duty as an educator to give my students the best possible training with the most up-to-date tools. I'm not alone in this opinion, either. Many civic groups donate software and hardware to these schools. They know the good job we're doing, and they know that we couldn't do a proper job without some degree of software copying.

What bothers me, though, is this: What are we teaching our students about the value of copyrights when they know we're using bootlegged copies, and they know we know it?

13

Test Data

Confidential or Dummy Data?

The Connecticut Cautionary Insurance Corporation (CCIC) is a multibillion-dollar life insurance company with over three million policyholders. J. William Willow heads CCIC's corporate Data Systems Development (DSD) Group. The DSD Group is responsible for producing and maintaining all programs that manage CCIC's insurance policies. Sybil Bonham heads a team of eight programmers who work in DSD as systems analysts. Their responsibilities include the analysis and design of many programs, and often their coding and maintenance.

Sybil, the lead analyst on the development of the insurance-policy service program, was recruited last year by Bill Willow to help the DSD Group improve the reliability of their software products. Sybil's leadership prompted the DSD Group to adopt several improved software engineering practices such as walkthroughs, top-down development, and structured techniques. She also recommended the automated test-data generation tools that the DSD Group now uses routinely. The Insurance Policy Service System, or IPSS, was the first software product developed using these tools and techniques.

Two weeks ago, the Whole Life Annuity Analysis Program, a part of IPSS, bombed on its first run on real data, and it took several hours to locate and fix the bug. Sybil went to the archive database to find the flaw that caused the program's failure. The error documentation file in the archive database showed that the instruction to calculate average annual gain divided the sum of interest by the policyholder's age in years. The real data had a case where the age of the policyholder was zero years.

Sybil explained to Bill Willow that her program had been tested to meet all the conditions she was told about. But she went on to explain that there was no way she could be sure that this covered all the conditions in the live data files. She concluded that she could produce a much more reliable program by testing it on live data from the policyholder file. Bill resisted, indicating that customer data was confidential information and was available only for production runs. Sybil explained that specification errors could not be generated with the test data software, that she could uncover these types of errors only by running her program against live data. Bill refused to allow this breach of the company's rules.

Sybil became angry. "Bill, you and I both know that if we had tested this program with live data from the policyholder file, we'd have discovered that specification error and probably many others besides. And we both know that the Group couldn't care less what the data represents. It can't be a breach of confidentiality if we don't look at the data, can it? Please, let us use live data and get this job done right."

Bill responded with equal force. "No. It's company policy, and I'm not going to let you compromise it. Run the program on the test data. If another specification error stops it, we'll correct that and repeat the process until we get it right."

One hour ago, the revised program ran for a third time against artificial test data, and passed again with no errors, but Sybil was still not convinced and again pleaded with Bill to allow a test on live data. After all, the Group had run the program on test data twice already, expecting flawless performance. But in both cases, the program crashed, forcing yet more changes.

Bill has a problem. His boss, the Vice President for Information Systems, has been pressuring him to get the Group to release the Whole Life Annuity Analysis program. He's irritated with Sybil for her constant pleas to use live data, and he feels stymied by the company policy. Somehow, he's got to get the project moving again. He is sorely tempted to follow Sybil's suggestion. He knows that if he does, he can get this program into production within the next week.

Bill calls Sybil into his office to discuss the program and its future testing. He says, "OK, here's what we do. . . ."

Case

14

The Brain Pick

A Knowledge-Based System Can't Know Everything

The Davis Stamp Company of Bismark, North Dakota is the second largest company in the world that caters to the needs of philatelists, or stamp collectors. It sells stamps, albums, catalogs, and every kind of accessory any collector could want. It has a reputation for fairly pricing its rare stamps, taking into consideration their condition and authenticating them as genuine when there is any doubt. Alex MacPhearson and Joan Andrews are two experts at Davis who are often called upon to judge the value and authenticity of especially rare stamps.

The Scan-Do Corporation of Phoenix, Arizona announced its Model 720 high-resolution flatbed color scanner last year. It won rave reviews from every critic. It is easy to use, can differentiate over 16 million shades, and has a resolution of 1,200 dots per inch. Although its cost exceeds $17,000, it is unique in the marketplace. Unfortunately, it hasn't been a big seller, in part because no one has developed a need for its high-quality features. Monica Burke's job at Scan-Do is to change that. She is a consultant engineer whose assignment is to develop the software for the expert system called PhilaTeller, an automated postage stamp evaluator.

Monica is in Bismark to meet with Alex and Joan of Davis Stamp and to work with them for two months. She is developing a computerized questionnaire that Alex and Joan, and any other philatelic expert, can answer to build the knowledge base for PhilaTeller. PhilaTeller is now in its infancy, containing as a database the entire contents of *Weston's United States Specialized Stamp Catalog*. If PhilaTeller works for the high-priced U.S. stamps, Scan-Do experts think that it can work for all other countries' stamps and for other stamp companies.

Because Monica is a stamp collector as well as a knowledge engineer, she feels confident that she can produce the questionnaire in less than the allowed time. For three weeks, Monica asks about dimensions and printing, perforation, color transfer, types, and gross and fine errors, from cracked plates to missing frame lines. Her questionnaire is developing nicely, but she begins to sense a reticence on the part of Alex and Joan. They occasionally seem vague in their answers.

Monica's next topic is paper. "What can I ask about the paper? Thickness? Color? Kind?"

Joan hesitates, then says, "I'm not sure I can word a question for you on that. Sometimes the paper just feels right, and sometimes I know it's wrong. It's not thickness, or transparency, or color, or anything like that. It's almost like . . . a feeling . . . something I just know—like you know that a strange dog is friendly. You don't know why, but something about it tells you it won't hurt you."

"What about you, Alex? Can you be more specific so that we can put it into question form?"

"Unfortunately, I agree with Joan. Oh, sure, some details are easy to measure, like thickness and color. But I seem to sense some qualities that I can only attribute to experience. For example, I can't tell exactly why I can differentiate parchment types from rag paper or thick paper types. I guess that's why Joan and I get big bucks for our judgments."

Monica frowns. She makes a few more attempts to get more information and then moves on to the next area. She feels that she can fill in the gaps herself.

Two years later, PhilaTeller is a trusted aide in judging incoming stamps from collections for several large companies and dealers. One day the following news story appears.

Dallas Register (UP)—Computer Fails to Spot Rare Stamp

Hortense Gneiss, of Hopewell Texas, is suing the Bondurance Stamp and Coin Company for $1,000,000 for failure to perform professionally and misrepresentation of their expertise. Ms. Gneiss alleges that an expert system called "PhilaTeller" did not correctly identify a Danish West Indies stamp she sold in a collection. Although Gneiss did not know it at the time of the sale, the stamp was what collectors call the "Three Palms Blue on Parchment." The stamp is unique, and supposedly worth in excess of $750,000 to collectors.

The collection, which she sold to Bondurance for $120,000, was later sold to the Davis Stamp Company of Bismark, North Dakota. The Three Palms Blue was discovered by Alex MacPhearson, who was working as a private consultant for the Davis Company. MacPhearson was helping to divide the collection into small job lots for easier sale.

The expert system, which is a program that is designed to act like an expert when fed the right questions, was developed by Scan-Do Corporation of Phoenix, Arizona. Representatives of Scan-Do could not be reached for comment.

Case

15

Trouble in Sardonia

Do Copyright Ethics Change Overseas?

Luke Atwater is on the fast track at JKL Corporation, headquartered in Dallas, Texas. JKL is a billion-dollar contractor for oil companies, specializing in heavy-duty oil-well drilling and pumping equipment. Luke's last job was to manage the start-up of a marketing branch in Chicago where, among other tasks, he was responsible for installing all hardware and software for the branch office. The office occupied the entire fifteenth floor, 23 rooms in all, of the Sears Tower. He had to network PCs for all offices with the appropriate productivity software. This included spreadsheet systems, word processing software, and a JKL Corporate Marketing Package. Luke completed the job in only four months, even though Pamela Courant, his immediate supervisor, had given him six months to do it. Pamela is the Corporate Vice President for Information Systems and Administration in Dallas.

Now Luke is in his next posting, in Russula, Sardonia, trying to repeat his stunning Chicago performance. He's been here for four months already, and practically nothing has happened, except that the old Wisteria Hotel has been remodeled into some semblance of an office building. He knows he's got to pick up the pace, or his job will be up for grabs.

Pamela told him over the phone before he left, "Luke, I expect more from you now. The Sardonia office is our first international office, and it could be the key to our international expansion. It has to be in the black—that means profitable, making us money—in six months. I'll give you those six months as I did in Chicago, but I expect you to do better than that."

Luke remembers his misgivings about being able to meet this newest deadline. Sardonia's pace is definitely slower than Chicago's, because of its easy-going culture and stifling bureaucracy. But he sees one unexpected compensation for the difficulties he has encountered: Sardonia's economy is far less developed than it could be. Anything JKL does for this country will be greatly appreciated and will reflect well on the company.

Luke expects no problems with the hardware. JKL managed the transshipment of all PCs from its headquarters in Dallas. All Luke had to do was to notify Pamela exactly how many PCs of what type, how big a central server, and how many feet of cable he needed. The shipment came in yesterday, and the parts are already being distributed. Luke knows that there will be some of the usual problems with wiring, but resolving them shouldn't take more than a week or two.

The real problem, Luke thinks to himself, is going to be the commercial software for word processing and spreadsheets. Pamela specifically requires that all JKL offices use Multisoft's MultiGrid and MultiWrite. Luke has been in phone contact with Multisoft for the past two days. He described to them the layout of the office, including the number of standalone PCs and those that would use a central server. He knew that in Chicago, the cost for site licenses for such a setup would be $40,000 for 100 to 249 users, and $75,000 for 250 to 499 users. He was surprised to learn that for international sites, including Sardonia, the costs are $90,000 and $175,000 respectively.

Luke calls in his software manager, Grifolo Frondoso, a native Sardonian familiar with both packages. "Grif, I want you to order MultiGrid and MultiWrite for our office. How many copies of each do you think you'll need?"

"Well, I should get at least 350 of each, if you expect this office to grow during the next year. We've got enough money budgeted for that. It shouldn't add up to more than about $2,000 U.S."

"I hate to give you the bad news, Grif, but JKL can't use low-grade word processing and spreadsheet software. It has to be Multisoft, and Multisoft wants $175,000 for that many users. That's way beyond the $90,000 our budget allows."

"That makes no sense, boss. We don't have to order from Multisoft here. I can get you copies of the exact same software for a dollar over the cost of the diskettes, all legal and above board."

"Sure, but that's not the latest release. And besides, that's copyrighted software. You can't do that."

"Yes, we can, here in Sardonia. The U.S. software copyright laws don't apply here. We can get as many copies as we want of the newest versions. Or, we could order one fresh copy from Multisoft and make copies."

"Even if we were to do that, we'd be without manuals. We've got to have manuals at each station, so that kills your idea. And don't forget future revisions . . ."

"No problem. We can copy the manuals too, or we can pay a local printer who needs the work to print high-quality copies for about $3 each. That still falls under the $90,000 limit, by about $88,000. And don't worry about revisions. We'll get them, too. Hey, just imagine your reputation when you deliver this site that far under budget."

Luke stands up and walks to the window overlooking Russula's oppressive slums, saying nothing. He's deep in thought for some time, then turns to Grifolo Frondoso and says, "Here's my decision. We'll . . ."

Bad Medicine

Well-Intentioned Software Could Cause Harm

Larry Indole was, until recently, in charge of computer security at InterGraf Corporation. InterGraf is located in Atlanta's high-tech suburbs; it is one of the three top graphics software providers in the world. Larry's job at InterGraf was to protect the company against any threats to its computer resources, especially its software and data. He had a reputation for being proactive in his work. He always tried to anticipate a problem before it happened, and provide a solution or preventive measure before any damage was done.

While Larry was still employed by InterGraf, he worked on his own computer at home on a pet project. It was an anti-virus program in which he took great pride. However, he soon realized that in order to increase the value of the program and to make it stand out from the competition, he would have to improve it to operate in a networked environment. When it came time for him to test this more powerful version of the program, he bought the extra hardware and software to create his own small linked set of computers. He dreamed of creating a start-up company that would market and upgrade his software for all users, no matter how complex.

Larry's program, which he called LIVID for Larry Indole's Virus Identifier and Destroyer, had several features that made it different and more attractive. It was very easy to use. It had:

- A sophisticated graphics user interface, or GUI
- Help screens and graphics for every activity
- Procedures for backing out of any potentially hazardous activity

It could recognize and destroy both old and new viruses. It could describe a virus in detail by type; by its effect on the system; by its source; and by its structure: it could display the source code of the virus. In addition, it allows the user to isolate the virus and copy it to a diskette. As proof that LIVID could destroy any new virus, it allows the user to modify an existing virus and then set LIVID loose on this new, redesigned version. LIVID destroys the new virus every time.

Larry suggested to InterGraf that the company use this product. He mentioned to his boss Gloria Gavilan that InterGraf had its share of infections, and could improve its security greatly by using LIVID. Larry told Gloria that he was willing to let the company buy the program at a discount, as a first customer.

Gloria had many misgivings about this program. She told Larry, "It looks to me as if you've developed an extremely dangerous program. If InterGraf were to make it available on the network, it would be like leaving a kid in a candy store. InterGraf won't buy this program, I promise you. In fact, I'm sure the company wouldn't take it if were free of charge. It's entirely too dangerous."

Larry was shocked. He considered his program to be an unquestion-able asset. How could Gloria take it upon herself to refuse it? He decided to make LIVID available on the Internet and give up his dreams of profit-ing from his work. Instead, he would become a consultant on the Internet, helping people use the program. The next day, he set up a BBS (bulletin board system) that would provide the program, both in executable and source form.

When Gloria discovered what Larry had done, she immediately fired him. Larry has now been out of a job for two weeks, during which time he advertised his new program on the Internet.

Ramon Gutierrez works as systems administrator at the Universidad Ciudad Mexico. He has followed LIVID's publicity on the Internet, and is considering the value of downloading it and using it at UCM. He approaches his boss and asks, "Should we download LIVID? I think it's a great idea. We're always infected with some virus, and our vaccine software can't seem to keep up. Also, the software we have is difficult to use. We can't disinfect our entire network at once, for example, which LIVID can do. What do you think?"

Code Blue

Patient Data at a Hospital Is Compromised

Metropolitan General Hospital is a large urban institution known for the efficient management of resources. The Information Systems department at MGH has been transitioning from a centralized to a distributed system. Presently, MGH uses its mainframe for most administrative, research, and patient-information databases. Access to this powerful system is through smart terminals and PCs acting as terminals. The PCs also act as standalone word processors and file managers at most sites throughout the hospital.

There are PCs at each nurses' station on each of the hospital's 20 floors. Each PC has software that can access the main system and download that station's present patient information. The nurses can interact with the PC to access patient data, thus reducing both response time and the load on the mainframe.

One of the busiest areas is on the third floor, West Wing. This is the Vehicular Accidents area. Only the most serious accident victims are brought to this ward; the simple concussions, lacerations, and broken limbs end up elsewhere. Here, every case is touch-and-go, requiring much attention and vigilance.

On her computer screen, Nurse Betty Blodgett has just brought up the record of Mr. Nathaniel Barker, the patient in room 15. She has a copy of the accident report at her desk, and is reading the medical record page by page. She discovers that Barker—age 37, 6 feet 3 inches tall, 170 pounds, and with a red beard—was riding his Harley Davidson at dusk heading east. He was about to start a gentle left turn when an approaching westbound Mercedes station wagon lost the curve in the setting sun. The head-on collision conformed to Newton's laws exactly. It slowed the big German car perceptibly, and it reversed the Harley's direction in 0.23 milliseconds.

Nurse Blodgett is absorbed in the scrolling medical report. After reading a page, she taps the spacebar, both to advance to the next page and to let the software know she's active at the keyboard. The Information Systems department has purposely designed all software that displays patient information to blank the screen and quit the job if the user doesn't interact in 60 seconds.

Suddenly, the intercom blares, "Code Blue room 23! Code Blue, room 23!"

Betty reacts immediately. She leaves at a run to get the crash cart and assist in room 23. She leaves the station unstaffed, but that's standard in an emergency.

Melody Burns is a volunteer who desperately wants to be a nurse. She has been helping out in the VA ward for a month now, comforting the patients in their agony, distributing ice water, fluffing pillows, and in general doing the simple tasks that so greatly help the nurses. She gets off the elevator to an empty station. But she heard the insistent Code Blue call, so she knows where they all are. She enters the nurses' station and sees the PC screen fully lit with a patient's record still on it. She scans it, thinking, "Ah, Mr. Barker! He's such a dear. Of course he can't talk, with his jaw wired and bandaged, but his eyes do tell so much. Let's see what his record says . . . He weighs 170 pounds? Gee, I'd have guessed even less, he's so thin . . . Appendix operation. Blood type A positive. HIV positive. What? HIV positive? My gosh, I had no idea. . . ." The screen blanks and Melody walks out of the nurses' station just as Nurse Blodgett returns.

"Melody! So glad to see you. We sure have had a busy afternoon. Mr. Barker's got his jaw working again, and he's asked to see you the minute you came in. He's so appreciative, as we all are, of the great work you've done. . . . Why, Mel, what's the matter?"

"I just can't see Mr. Barker anymore. I'm sorry. It's just that, well . . . maybe I've been spending too much time with him at the expense of the other patients. And besides, I can't get too close to him. I might get AIDS."

Betty is shocked. "What do you mean? What makes you think something like that?"

Case

18

Virtual Success

Virtual-Reality Games Invade the Real World

Planet Studios, like the major studios with which it competes, is a conglomerate made up of many companies that supply the entertainment industry with everything from silver for film to people as contract actors. It includes theater chains, movie and TV hardware, entertainment parks, and even a high-tech research center. Planet's FX Group, located on a 3,500-acre ranch outside Santa Monica, started out 10 years ago as a small lab with 12 engineers. Now, with 285 employees, it is a major manufacturer of high-tech entertainment hardware, such as arcade games and home entertainment accessories.

The latest product to come out of FX Group is a series of virtual-reality, or VR, arcade games. Much R&D effort went into this product, and it seems to be paying off. The two games FX has released for sale are GTP, a simulation of a high-performance race car at the Limerock Race Track in Connecticut, and Real Flight, which simulates the takeoff, flight, and landing of a Piper Cherokee from Meigs Field in Chicago. Both games supply all the sensory data—sight, sound, G forces, even the smell of fuel and burning rubber. The price of these game machines is high, but demand for them is encouraging.

FX is successful, but trapped in a financial squeeze of its own creation. To get its leading-edge position in the marketplace, the designers of the VR games were always encouraged to use the best hardware to make the sensory cues as real as possible. The present models use four RISC processors, but the competition still uses microprocessors of a more traditional design. The added processors make the FX product functionally superior, but greatly reduce the profit margin. FX is looking for a "cash cow," a highly profitable product or a major long-term contract. That will allow the group to balance the budget and provide future growth.

Julia Parker is President and Chief Executive Officer of FX. She has called a meeting with Michael LaPlante, VP of Future Projects, and Jim Wall, lead programmer and technical wizard in the Future Projects department. The three are to meet with Ted MacDonald, who is Chief of Technical Support for the FBI Training Facility in Quantico, Virginia. None of the three FX people know exactly what Mr. MacDonald will propose, but they chat informally in the board room with high hopes that maybe this is the break they've been looking for, a government contract.

Mr. MacDonald is ushered in, and after a round of introductions and the ubiquitous coffee, he presents his proposal. "The FBI needs versions of your arcade games, but modified so that they can be used in realistic training situations rather than for entertainment. We want . . ." Ted MacDonald uses overhead transparencies to display the FBI's needs:

- A variant of Real Flight, but with a helicopter, in different settings (such as city and country, day and night).

- A variant of GTP, except using an armored personnel carrier in counter-terrorist settings. This product will train agents to use the machine guns and 40-millimeter cannon, and accustom them to being shot at.

- A new product to provide small-arms training against realistic foes who mix with innocent civilians. This product will be more realistic than current models used for the same purpose and will save lives.

After answering many questions, Mr. MacDonald leaves for Quantico. He expects a decision within the week.

The meeting in the board room is now much more uninhibited between the three remaining FX people. Jim Wall says, "It can be done, and easily. Both GTP and Real Flight are based on the same internal hardware. It makes no difference to the hardware whether we're landing an airplane or shooting someone. It will take some intense programming, but that's what they'll pay us the big bucks for, right?"

Michael LaPlante's enthusiasm is less evident. "I'm worried about the FBI's third proposal. I just don't like the idea of training people to kill, even if it's in their line of duty. I could go along with one and two, though, as long as we concentrate on the look and feel of the settings, and don't get into 'taking out targets,' as the man said in his presentation."

Julia Parker must make the final decision. She must weigh the assured success of the company if it takes on the FBI proposal against a risky, possibly doomed future if FX continues on its present course.

His Private Lab

A Student Tries to Justify Computer Use

Cast of Characters

Professor Williams, instructor in Business Information Systems, a junior-senior-level course at Bryce College
Students:
  Angela
  Benjamin
  Charlene
  Dwight
  Erica
  Francis
  Gladys
  Harry

Prof.	Well done, class. In general, your grasp of the essentials of advanced spreadsheet design seems quite good. However, some of you seem to have strong feelings about one question I asked you on the previous assignment, the one concerning Bryce's ethics policy. Turn to your answer to Question 9. Angela, would you please read the question?
Angela	If you as a student at Bryce are selling your own homemade fast food as a part-time job to pay your tuition, is it OK for you to use your copy of the Exceed 1-2-3 program in Bryce's computer lab to do your accounting? Why or why not?
Prof.	All right, let's discuss this question. Who wants to start? . . . Ben?
Benjamin	No, it's not OK. Because you're using the college's computer.
Charlene	So what's wrong with that? Aren't we supposed to learn how to use the computer? That's the purpose of the lab, isn't it? To give us the facilities to learn.
Dwight	Sure, that's its purpose, but the question says the part-time job is helping you to pay tuition, so it's a profit-making concern. The lab is intended to support your educational needs, not your financial needs.

Erica	Suppose it means to the student the difference between attending Bryce and dropping out for a year. Isn't that a good reason for using the lab?
Gladys	You're overlooking something. What if all the students at Bryce were to use the lab for their part-time jobs so that they could meet their tuition bills? We'd never be able to get in there to do our normal school assignments.
Francis	Bad argument, Gladys. Everybody's not doing it. I mean, not everyone at Bryce needs to work part-time to pay their tuition. Professor Williams, what about polling the class to see how many here are working at all . . . I mean, how many have to work to be able to stay here as students?
Prof.	I'm afraid I can't do that. Tell you what, though. Suppose everyone of you think of a student acquaintance here at Bryce but not in this class, and respond as if you were that acquaintance. You don't have to identify this person, only respond as if you were that person. Now, how many of you (think of yourselves as that other person) are working either part-time or full-time in order to pay your bills at Bryce? Let's see . . . three, four, . . . , seven, eleven. . . . Looks like about half of you. Erica, back to you.
Erica	Well, I see that even though not one hundred percent of the students have to work, there are still enough to really impact the system. But they don't have to do their computer work during peak hours, do they? I mean, if I were a student who had a job on the side, and if it was the only way I could stay at Bryce, I'd use the lab, sure, but only when I wouldn't interfere with any student doing her schoolwork.
Benjamin	Yeah, and besides, probably most of the students who have to work on the side wouldn't need to use the computer lab, anyway. So lots less than half, probably only one in ten, would benefit from the lab's hardware.
Dwight	Professor, that phrase in the question—to use your copy of the Exceed 1-2-3 program—is it referring to a program I've bought for myself from the vendor, or is it the Bryce College Student Version? I mean, that version is . . . what's the word? crippled . . . so that it really isn't like a real version. . . .

Angela	Of course, it's a real version. You just don't have all the bells and whistles, but you have all any small business might need, and that's what we're talking about.
Benjamin	Not only that, but you got it at a ridiculously low price, roughly a tenth of what the commercial version costs, because Bryce signed an agreement with Exceed so that we could have it. Of course, Exceed is happy to do the deal, because we'll get familiar with their version of spreadsheeting, so we're more likely to buy their commercial version when we get a job.
Gladys	Somehow, I tend to think it's OK for Bryce to restrict the use of the lab to school-related use only. Why shouldn't they?
Prof.	Gladys, what do you mean, "restrict the use"? Where is there such a restriction?
Erica	The Bryce College Statement of Ethical Computer Use says, uh, let's see, here it is: "The computer facilities at Bryce are intended solely for the support of an individual's primary endeavors as a student or employee of Bryce College." A student's primary endeavors are educational, not professional. A student should be studying, doing assignments, and so on. Working isn't a part of being a student, is it?
Charlene	It sure is part of being a student, if you have to work to get your bills paid so that you can stay in school. I think it's fine for a student to use his or her own copy of software in the lab, when a computer is free to use, as long as he or she is willing to give it up to a student who has schoolwork.
Francis	Oh, yeah, sure! I can just see you tapping our football team's tackle on the shoulder while he's doing his books in the lab, and telling him to leave the computer because you want to practice some Exceed commands.
Charlene	All right, I see your point. So I don't use the lab unless there are at least five free computers. That still happens a lot, so I'd get my work done, and nobody would get hurt, and I'd be able to stay at Bryce because I could afford its tuition.
Gladys	Even so, Charlene, you'd be misusing the resources. You'd be stealing computer time, and you'd be taking the risk of seriously damaging something. Suppose, for example, the

system crashes while you're doing your bookkeeping for your job? You've just knocked out a computer, which could be important during the next busy time. And would you expect the college to compensate you for your lost data?

Prof.   We'll have to cut off discussion now. Before we do, does anyone who hasn't spoken have anything to add?

Harry   Yessir, I do. We've been talking about Bryce's ethics policy, and your "Is it OK?" question. But that still doesn't solve my problem. I work as a lab assistant here at Bryce, which helps me out some when it comes time to pay tuition. For the past three and a half years, I've been developing a small desktop publishing business on the side. I bought my own copy of the desktop publishing software I use, and I use my own hardware almost exclusively. That business, along with the lab assistant job, has let me stay as a student at Bryce.

Now, my problem is this: My own computer is four years old, and I can't afford to upgrade it to do the things I need to do to keep my present customers. So I've been using my lab key to get into it between 2 and 3 A.M. for the past three months, so that I could use the new workstation there. No one has ever complained, mostly because no one knew. I always leave the machine as I found it, and I'm extra careful with it.

There are six weeks left in this semester, and I haven't paid the tuition for this semester yet. And if I can keep using that workstation, I can graduate. Otherwise, I have to drop out.

[Professor Williams *scratches his head. He seems at a loss for words.*]

Prof.   Class dismissed. Harry, let's go to my office. We'll talk.

Appendix

Ethics Codes
and Policies

THE NEED FOR CODES AND POLICIES

One of the essential steps in creating an ethical computing environment is establishing rules of conduct. This includes defining the organizational expectations of how computer users will act as well as defining how computer professionals will perform their duties. There are variations in how organizations want their employees to use computers, but in any approach the overriding principle when seeking appropriate computer use should be informed consent. The users should be *informed* of the rules, and by agreeing to use the system on that basis, *consent* to abide by the rules.

The typical way to establish and promulgate rules for appropriate computer use is through codes of conduct and policies. These take many forms and vary from organization to organization. Indeed, many organizations do not even have codes or policies. The wise organization will have codes and policies as well as a process for their periodic review and updating. It will make a conscientious effort to make the users aware of the codes and policies, through formal training and other means. This will best serve the user, both professional and nonprofessional, and the organization. The user will know how to act, and if things go wrong the organization will have a published standard through which to deal with the infraction.

The following sections describe two codes and two policies that could serve as guides for an organization seeking to establish or revisit rules for its environment. The first code is specifically directed to information systems professionals, while the others apply to all users of a computer system. Though the latter three were developed for an academic environment, they can be models for any kind of organization, for they were written to apply not only to students but also to faculty, staff, and administrators.

The Association for Computing Machinery (ACM) Code of Ethics and Professional Conduct

The Association for Computing Machinery (ACM) is a professional organization of more than 80,000 computer professionals, academics, and students. It is by far the largest computer organization of its type, and its purpose is to foster understanding about information technology and standards for its use. The ACM has had a code of conduct for many years; it was last revised in 1992. Other computer professional organizations, such as the Data Processing Management Association (DPMA), the Institute of Electrical and Electronic Engineers (IEEE), the Canadian Information Processing Society (CIPS), and the British Computer Society (BCS), have similar codes.

These codes serve a useful purpose in clarifying the responsibility of the membership to act in appropriate ways in regard to computer system development and use. They have two shortcomings, however. First, they are addressed to professional organization membership. With the proliferation of computers throughout an enterprise, it is conceivable that only a small fraction of those using information technology will be information systems professionals and members of such organizations as the ACM. And second, the code is advisory at best. The organization cannot impose sanctions on those who violate it, except perhaps the cancellation of membership.

The best way for an information systems department to use these codes is to adopt one of the codes as its own, inform employees that behavior is expected to be in accordance with the code, and that violations will be punished. Then the department should set about developing one or more additional specific codes or policies that meet its particular circumstances. The codes and policies should also apply to nonprofessionals who use computers and participate in the development of computer applications.

ACM CODE OF ETHICS AND PROFESSIONAL CONDUCT

> On October 16, 1992, ACM's Executive Council voted to adopt a revised Code of Ethics.

Commitment to ethical professional conduct is expected of every voting, associate, and student member of ACM. This Code, consisting of 24 imperatives formulated as statements of personal responsibility, identifies the elements of such a commitment.

It contains many, but not all, issues professionals are likely to face. Section 1 outlines fundamental ethical considerations, while Section 2 addresses additional, more specific considerations of professional conduct. Statements in Section 3 pertain more specifically to individuals who have a leadership role, whether in the workplace or in a volunteer capacity, for example with organizations such as ACM. Principles involving compliance with this Code are given in Section 4.

The Code is supplemented by a set of Guidelines, which provide explanation to assist members in dealing with the various issues contained in the Code. It is expected that the Guidelines will be changed more frequently than the Code. See Anderson, et al., 1993, for more detail.

The Code and its supplemented Guidelines are intended to serve as a basis for ethical decision making in the conduct of professional work. Secondarily, they may serve as a basis for judging the merit of a formal complaint pertaining to violation of professional ethical standards.

It should be noted that although computing is not mentioned in the moral imperatives section, the Code is concerned with how these fundamental imperatives apply to one's conduct as a computing professional. These imperatives are expressed in a general form to emphasize that ethical principles which apply to computer ethics are derived from more general ethical principles.

It is understood that some words and phrases in a code of ethics are subject to varying interpretations, and that any ethical principle may conflict with other ethical principles in specific situations. Questions related to ethical conflicts can be answered by thoughtful consideration of fundamental principles, rather than reliance on detailed regulations.

1.   General Moral Imperatives

As an ACM member I will . . .

1.1   Contribute to society and human well-being
1.2   Avoid harm to others
1.3   Be honest and trustworthy
1.4   Be fair and take action not to discriminate
1.5   Honor property rights including copyrights and patents
1.6   Give proper credit for intellectual property
1.7   Respect the privacy of others
1.8   Honor confidentiality

2.   More Specific Professional Responsibilities

As an ACM computing professional I will . . .

2.1   Strive to achieve the highest quality, effectiveness and dignity in both the process and products of professional work
2.2   Acquire and maintain professional competence
2.3   Know and respect existing laws pertaining to professional work
2.4   Accept and provide appropriate professional review
2.5   Give comprehensive and thorough evaluations of computer systems and their impacts, with special emphasis on possible risks

2.6   Honor contracts, agreements, and assigned responsibilities

2.7   Improve public understanding of computing and its consequences

2.8   Access computing and communication resources only when authorized to do so

3. Organizational Leadership Imperatives

As an ACM member and an organizational leader, I will . . .

3.1   Articulate social responsibilities of members of an organizational unit and encourage full acceptance of those responsibilities

3.2   Manage personnel and resources to design and build information systems that enhance the quality of working life

3.3   Acknowledge and support proper and authorized uses of an organization's computing and communication resources

3.4   Ensure that users and those who will be affected by a system have their needs clearly articulated during the assessment and design of requirements. Later the system must be validated to meet requirements.

3.5   Articulate and support policies that protect the dignity of users and others affected by a computing system

3.6   Create opportunities for members of the organization to learn the principles and limitations of computer systems

4. Compliance with the Code

As an ACM member, I will . . .

4.1   Uphold and promote the principles of this Code

4.2   Treat violations of this Code as inconsistent with membership in the ACM

A Code for Ethical Computer Use

A code for ethical computer use serves much like the U.S. Constitution. It espouses general principles to guide computer user behavior. This avoids having to change the code with each technological update, but it also requires some interpretation on the part of the user. For example, one section of the code on page 113 reads as follows:

The fundamental purpose of the college computer resource is to support an individual's primary endeavors as a student or employee of the college.

Does this statement allow game playing? The answer is not always clear. For students, game playing is probably allowed since part of the educational objective is to overcome fear of computers and make the student comfortable with technology. Game playing has been shown to do this. But for an administrative employee, this might be considered a waste of the organization's time. When a student plays games, the only cost to the organization is computer time. When an employee plays, there is the computer cost as well as the person cost.

With a code written in this high-level manner, some effort must be made to teach those who come under the code how to evaluate their actions in light of the code. If they are unable do it themselves, specific guidance to one in authority must be provided. The former is accommodated with training sessions, in the classroom for the students, and as part of employee orientation for others. The code also specifically states whom to ask for guidance if the user in is doubt about an action. Furthermore, the code should be published in organization bulletins and displayed prominently in computer work areas. Some organizations have their users sign a document stating that they understand and agree to the code. Other organizations deny system access until the user reads and agrees to the code electronically through the initial sign-on process. The code should clearly state that sanctions will be imposed if its provisions are not followed.

If the organization has only one code or policy, it must be a Code for Ethical Computer Use. This is the starting point and also the umbrella for any other guides that may be established.

CODE FOR ETHICAL COMPUTER USE*

Introduction

All members of the college community, students, faculty, staff, and administration have opportunities to use computers and be affected by computer usage in the pursuit of their primary endeavors at the college.

Therefore, it is critical that such computer use be performed in an ethical context which ensures that the use of these resources fosters the achievement of the individual user's goals, consistent with college educational and research objectives.

Such an ethical context implies that computing resources will not be abused, wasted, or employed in such a way as to interfere with, or cause harm or damage to another person, institution, or company within or outside the college community. It is up to the individual to act responsibly in the use of computer hardware and software, data and computer outputs.

Policy Statement

The fundamental purpose of the college computer resource is to support an individual's primary endeavors as a student or employee of the college.

An individual may only use accounts, files, software and computer resources authorized under his/her particular password.

Individuals must take all reasonable precautions (e.g., prevent unauthorized access to accounts or data by others) both within and outside the college community.

Individuals must not make unauthorized copies of copyrighted software or data. An employee's questions of copyright provisions or permissions should be directed

---

*The Code for Ethical Computer Use, E-Mail Privacy Policy, and Internet Use Policy are based on those in place at Bentley College, Waltham, MA.

to his or her supervisor or the supervisor of the computing facility. A student's questions should be addressed to a member of the faculty or the supervisor of the computing facility.

Employees are expected to report to their supervisors or the supervisor of the computing facility, and students are expected to report to a faculty member or the supervisor of the computing facility, any violations, flaws or other deficiencies in the security of any and all college computer resources.

Individuals must not abuse the college's computing resources so as to reduce their efficiency to the detriment of other users.

Individuals must not attempt to modify system facilities, utilities, and/or configurations, or change the restrictions associated with their accounts, or attempt to breach the college's computer resources security system, whether with or without malicious intent.

Individuals must not use any network access provided by the college to affect other computers or the network in any of the above ways.

If uncertain about a specific situation, an employee should consult a superior or supervisor; a student should consult a member of the faculty before proceeding.

Violations of this policy will be handled in a manner consistent with comparable situations requiring disciplinary action.

An E-Mail Privacy Policy

Electronic mail (e-mail) is so pervasive in the organizations that use it that it requires its own specific policy. This policy is more of an explanation of organizational actions than it is an attempt to direct user behavior. The major problem with e-mail is the user's expectation of privacy. To a large extent, this expectation is based on the false assumption that e-mail privacy protection is somehow analogous to U.S. first-class mail. This is simply not true. The misunderstanding is probably caused by the use of the word "mail" in both cases. So, if e-mail is not as private as U.S. mail, how private is it? That all depends.

Generally, under U.S. law, the organization that owns an internal e-mail system can operate that system as openly or as privately as it wishes. That means that if the organization wants to read everyone's e-mail, it can do so. If it chooses not to read any, that is allowable too. Hence, it is up to the organization to decide how much, if any, e-mail it is going to read. Then, when it decides, it must *inform* the users, so that they can *consent* to this level of intrusion. In other words, they will use the system knowing the extent to which their e-mail messages may be read by others. Although the sample policy that follows is on the high side of total privacy, the authors are more interested in urging organizations to have some kind of e-mail privacy policy and to publish it no matter what the degree of intrusion.

Some salient points about the sample policy:

1. The policy is complementary to the Code for Ethical Computer Use.

2. It defines who legitimate e-mail users are.

3. It explains the backup procedure so users will know that at some point, even if a message is deleted at the terminal, it will still be on the backup tapes.

4. It describes the legitimate grounds for reading someone's e-mail and the process required before such action can be taken.

5. It informs that the organization has no control of e-mail once it is transmitted outside.

6. It explains what will happen if the user severs his or her connection with the organization.

7. It asks employees to be careful to make any files and documents that pertain to an organization's business available to others who need them. This is the only action the policy asks of the user.

ELECTRONIC MAIL PRIVACY POLICY*
Introduction

This memorandum sets forth the college policy with regard to access to and disclosure of electronic mail (e-mail) messages sent or received by college employees, students, or other authorized parties with the use of the college's electronic mail system.

It also sets forth policies on the proper use of the electronic mail system provided by the college.

The college provides electronic mail to employees and students at the college's expense, for their use on college business and incidentally for personal purposes, so long as it does not violate college policy or adversely affect others.

The college's electronic mail system may be used by customers, suppliers and other third parties under certain circumstances if they agree to abide by all applicable rules.

The college copies e-mail files daily to backup tapes which are held for an indefinite period. Users should be aware that deletion of an electronic message in their mail folder will not delete a previously archived copy of that message.

The college intends to honor these policies but must reserve the right to change them at any time with such prior notices, if any, as may be reasonable under the circumstance.

Policy Statement

The college recognizes that e-mail users have a substantial interest in privacy with regard to the e-mail messages they send or receive. The following policy describes the degree of privacy e-mail users may reasonably assume.

*The Code for Ethical Computer Use, E-Mail Privacy Policy, and Internet Use Policy are based on those in place at Bentley College, Waltham, MA.

The college will not read or make available for anyone else to read the contents of any employee's, student's or authorized party's e-mail files without the permission of the user unless it has reasonable grounds to do so. Such grounds might include, but are not limited to, maintaining system integrity (such as tracking viruses), meeting legal obligations (such as subpoenas), and performing certain system management functions (such as routing misaddressed messages). However, under extraordinary circumstances, the college may access and disclose the contents of a user's e-mail messages, only with the approval of the Vice President of Information Services and the appropriate divisional Vice President. In such cases, the user will be notified as soon as practicable.

Employees should take steps to assure that college documents stored electronically that should be available to other employees of the college are so available.

The ability of the college to invoke privacy protection is limited to the on-campus network and does not extend to organizations or parties outside the college (i.e., through Bitnet or the Internet), where the policies of those entities, if any, apply.

When an e-mail user leaves the college, all personal e-mail messages should be deleted. The college reserves the right, however, to review any remaining active messages for their value in carrying out college business.

The policies described herein apply to both electronic mail currently stored on-line as well as archived files.

This policy complements the college Code for Ethical Computer Use, all provisions of which apply to e-mail users.

An Internet Use Policy

Like electronic mail, the Internet has some unique aspects that make it a good candidate for its own policy. These include the large amount of computing resources that Internet users can expend, thus making it essential that such use be legitimate. In addition, the Internet contains numerous materials that some might feel are offensive and, hence, some regulation might be required in this area. Furthermore, questions arise as to the intellectual property rights of the creators of many of the documents found on the Internet, so that some system must be invoked to ensure that users give proper credit to those creators. Hence, the sample Internet policy that follows is more directed toward guiding behavior than explaining organization action.

Some salient points of the Internet Use Policy:

1. It describes available Internet services. Not all Internet sites allow users to access all services.

2. It defines the organization's position on the purpose of Internet access and what restrictions, if any, are placed on that access. In this case, the policy is open access to encourage the free exchange of ideas.

3. The policy is complementary to the Code for Ethical Computer Use and other codes and policies of the organization.

4. It describes user responsibility for citing sources, properly handling offensive material, using the resource consistent with one's primary endeavor, and protecting the organization's good name.

5. Sanctions are called for if the policy is violated.

INTERNET USE POLICY*
Internet Definition:

The Internet is a loosely organized network encompassing hundreds of thousands of computers throughout the world located in academic, commercial, governmental and organizational sites. There is no central governing body overseeing the network's operation.

Some Internet Capabilities:

1. E-mail to virtually anyone on an Internet node.
2. Telnet—a direct connection to remote computers on the Internet, providing access to files, indices and other information resources at those locations.
3. File Transfer Protocol (FTP)—a procedure which enables copying of files between computing systems at different Internet locations.
4. News Groups—thousands of electronic discussion groups through which messages are disseminated to subscribing users at Internet locations.

Purpose in Providing Internet Access:

The Internet has the potential to be a valuable educational and research resource. Its communication capabilities can substitute for more expensive and slower alternatives. Its data access opportunities offer the advantage of speed as well as access to sources and information not available elsewhere. Finally, it offers the opportunity for an entirely new way of communicating, discussing, exploring, researching and interacting consistent with the technologies that are and will be available to graduates in their employment settings.

Principles Supporting Open Internet Access:

As stated above, the Internet is a useful educational and research tool. However, certain Internet services contain material which may be controversial. In principle, the college is opposed to censoring such material on the belief that the mission of the institution is best served by free and open discussion. Although access is open to all users, the individual still selects the manner of use. Thus, the college will hold users accountable for their individual behavior.

This principle is consistent with article 2 of the Library Bill of Rights:

Libraries should provide books and other materials presenting all points of view concerning the problems and issues of our times; no library mate-

---

*The Code for Ethical Computer Use, E-Mail Privacy Policy, and Internet Use Policy are based on those in place at Bentley College, Waltham, MA.

rials should be proscribed or removed from libraries because of partisan or doctrinal disapproval.

Guidelines for Internet Use:

The provisions of the Code for Ethical Computer Use, the Policy on E-mail Privacy, and the Academic Honesty Code and related policies apply to all Internet use and users. In addition, all users, faculty, students and staff, have additional responsibilities when using the Internet, due to the unique capabilities of that resource.

1. Responsibility for acknowledging source(s):

    Documents and other information accessed through the Internet which are used in compiling reports, term papers, journal articles and the like must be cited with a proper footnote and bibliographic reference as if the source were a book or other printed work. To do otherwise constitutes plagiarism and will be disciplined as such.

2. Responsibility for handling potentially offensive material with discretion:

    Material can be accessed on the Internet which some may consider to be objectionable or offensive. In no way does the college encourage or endorse accessing such material except for legitimate academic purposes.

    Users must exercise judgment when choosing the information they access. If there is the reasonable expectation that the accessed information would be considered objectionable by some, then public terminals (those in open offices, labs, the library and other public places) may not be used, and hardcopy of such information may not be directed to public printers.

    Thus, in accessing such material, the user has the responsibility to do so in a private environment, such as a dormitory room or private office, and in such a way that the material does not negatively affect those who deem it objectionable or offensive. As one example, such material should not be forwarded to others without their consent.

3. Responsibility for Internet use consistent with one's objectives as student, faculty or staff member:

    The college provides Internet capabilities to employees and students at the college's expense, for their use on college business and incidentally for personal purposes, so long as it does not violate college policy or adversely affect others. The Internet is not to be used to cause harm, no matter how minor, to any individual or computer facility. Prohibited activities include, but are not limited to: subscribing another person to a bulletin board or discussion group, planting or distributing viruses, using or distributing unauthorized software or sending harassing messages. Users are expected to act so as to always protect the college's good name and reputation.

Enforcement:

Violations of this policy will be handled in a manner consistent with comparable situations requiring disciplinary action.

ANNOTATED REFERENCES

Anderson, R. E., et al. Using the new ACM code of ethics in decision making, *Communications of the ACM,* February1993, 98–107.

A detailed explanation of the code and its application to nine specific scenarios.

Johnson, D. R., and J. Podesta. *Access to and Use and Disclosure of Electronic Mail on Company Computer Systems: A Tool Kit for Formulating Your Company's Policy,* Arlington, VA: Electronic Messaging (Mail) Association, 1991.

A step-by-step guide to e-mail privacy policy formulation. Especially useful in its suggestions of how to determine organizational attitudes on which policy is based.

Kallman, E. A. Developing a code for ethical computer use, *Journal of Systems and Software,* January 1992, 69–74.

A guide to the process and politics of creating an ethics code for a college.

Worksheets for the Four-Step Analysis Process

This section contains sets of blank worksheets designed to guide the reader through the four-step analysis process. The worksheet sections correspond to Figure 3-1 and the entries in the sample case analysis in Chapter 3. For convenient reference, Figure 1-1, Approaches to Ethical Decision Making, has been reproduced on the reverse of page 1 of the worksheet. Students may find the worksheet a helpful tool, even if the instructor does not formally assign it.

A workable approach to case analysis using the worksheet is for the instructor to assign just page 1 of the worksheet first, asking students to complete that page at home. In the next class, the instructor and students can review Steps I and II to reach agreement on facts, issues, stakeholders, and *the issue to be resolved now.* It is important, before going on to Step III, that everyone in the class is analyzing the same issue.

When the class agrees on the facts, stakeholders, and issues, the instructor can assign pages 3 and 4 of the worksheet. At the top of page 3, Step II is repeated so that students can enter the now agreed-upon issue, and proceed with the analysis from that point.

(Instructors: See the *Instructor's Manual* for more detail on assignments and case analysis.)

A FOUR-STEP ANALYSIS PROCESS

The legal assessment and application of guidelines have helped you to discover that something in this situation requires a closer look. Using this worksheet carry out each step of the analysis process to resolve the ethical dilemma. Refer to the explanation in Chapter 3 for details.

Step I. Understanding the situation

A. List and number the relevant facts.

> *Number*   *Fact*

> _____   _____
> _____   _____
> _____   _____
> _____   _____
> _____   _____
> _____   _____
> _____   _____
> _____   _____

B. Which of these raises an ethical issue? Why? What is the potential or resulting harm?

> *Fact* (number)   *Potential or resulting harm*

> [__] _____
> [__] _____
> [__] _____
> [__] _____
> [__] _____

C. List the stakeholders involved.

> _____
> _____
> _____
> _____

Step II. Isolating the major ethical dilemma

What is the ethical dilemma to be resolved NOW?

State it using the form: Should **someone** do or not do **something**? Note: Just state the dilemma here; leave any reasoning for Step III.

> _____
> _____
> _____

1

Figure 3-1
Approaches to Ethical Decision Making

Law and Ethics

Does the law provide an answer? (Professional help should be sought.)

Guidelines

Informal Guidelines

1. Is there something you or others would prefer to keep quiet?
   Are there "shushers" in the situation? Who wants to keep things quiet?
   Does it pass the Mom Test: Would you tell her? Would she do it?
   Does it pass the TV Test: Would you tell a nationwide audience?
   Does it pass the Market Test: Could you advertise the activity to gain a market edge?

2. Does your instinct tell you that something is wrong?
   Does it pass the Smell Test: Does the situation "smell"?

Formal Guidelines

1. Does the act violate corporate policy?
2. Does the act violate corporate or professional codes of conduct or ethics?
3. Does the act violate the Golden Rule?

Ethical Principles

Rights and Duties (deontology)

Are any rights abridged?
   The right to know
   The right to privacy
   The right to property

Are any duties or responsibilities not met?

Personal duties:
   • Trust   • Integrity   • Truthfulness   • Gratitude and reparation
   • Justice   • Beneficence and nonmaleficence   • Self-improvement

Professional duties (responsibilities)
   For all professionals:
      Maintain appropriate professional relationships
      Maintain efficacy
   For information professionals in particular:
      Maintain confidentiality
      Maintain impartiality

Consequentialism (teleology)

Does the action minimize actual and potential harm?

   Egoism: good for me, least harm to me
   Utilitarianism: good for the group, least harm for the group
   Altruism: good for all, some harm to me

Kant's Categorical Imperative

The principle of consistency: What if everyone acted this way?
The principle of respect: Are people treated as ends rather than means?

Step II. Isolating the major ethical dilemma What is the ethical dilemma to be resolved NOW? State it using the form: Should **someone** do or not do **something**? (Repeated from page 1.)

_____

_____

_____

Step III. Analyzing the ethicality of both alternatives in Step II

Consequentialism

    A. If action in Step II is done, who, if anyone, will be harmed? _____

    B. If action in Step II is not done, who, if anyone, will be harmed? _____

    C. Which alternative results in the least harm, A or B? [ ] A   [ ] B

    D. If action in Step II is done, who, if anyone, will benefit?   _____

    E. If action in Step II is not done, who, if anyone, will benefit? _____

    F. Which alternative results in the maximum benefit, D or E? [ ] D   [ ] E

Rights and Duties

    G. What **rights** have been or may be abridged? What **duties** have been or may be neglected? Identify the stakeholder and the right or duty. When listing a right, show its corresponding duty and vice versa.

_____

_____

_____

_____

_____

Kant's Categorical Imperative

    H. If action in Step II is done, who, if anyone, will be treated with *dis*respect? _____

    I. If action in Step II is not done, who, if anyone, will be treated with *dis*respect? _____

    J. Which alternative is preferable, H or I? [ ] H   [ ] I

    K. If action in Step II is done, who, if anyone, will be treated *un*like others? _____

    L. If action in Step II is not done, who, if anyone will be treated *un*like others? _____

    M. Which alternative is preferable, K or L? [ ] K   [ ] L

    N. Are there benefits if everyone did action in Step II? _____

    O. Are there benefits if nobody did action in Step II? _____

    P. Which alternative is preferable, N or O? [ ] N   [ ] O

Name _____ Class _____ Date _____ Case # _____

Step IV. Making a decision and planning the implementation

A. Make a defensible ethical decision.

Based on the analysis in Step III, answer the question in Step II. Indicate the letters of the categories that best support your response. Add any arguments justifying your choice of these ethical principles to support your decision. Where there are conflicting rights and duties, choose and defend those that take precedence. (Note: Just make and justify your choice here; leave any action steps for parts B and D below.)

_____
_____
_____

B. List the specific steps needed to implement your defensible ethical decision.

_____
_____
_____
_____
_____
_____

C. Show how the major stakeholders are affected by these actions.

_____
_____
_____
_____
_____

D. What other longer-term changes (political, legal, technical, societal, organizational) would help prevent such problems in the future?

_____
_____
_____
_____
_____

E. What should have been done or not done in the first place (at the pivot point) to avoid this dilemma?

_____
_____
_____
_____

4

Name _____ Class _____ Date _____ Case # _____

A FOUR-STEP ANALYSIS PROCESS

The legal assessment and application of guidelines have helped you to discover that something in this situation requires a closer look. Using this worksheet carry out each step of the analysis process to resolve the ethical dilemma. Refer to the explanation in Chapter 3 for details.

Step I. Understanding the situation

A. List and number the relevant facts.

Number   *Fact*

_____   _____
_____   _____
_____   _____
_____   _____
_____   _____
_____   _____
_____   _____
_____   _____

B. Which of these raises an ethical issue? Why? What is the potential or resulting harm?

Fact (number)   *Potential or resulting harm*

[__] _____
[__] _____
[__] _____
[__] _____
[__] _____

C. List the stakeholders involved.

_____
_____
_____
_____

Step II. Isolating the major ethical dilemma

What is the ethical dilemma to be resolved NOW?

State it using the form: Should **someone** do or not do **something**? Note: Just state the dilemma here; leave any reasoning for Step III.

_____
_____
_____

Figure 3-1
Approaches to Ethical Decision Making

Law and Ethics

Does the law provide an answer? (Professional help should be sought.)

Guidelines

Informal Guidelines

1. Is there something you or others would prefer to keep quiet?
> Are there "shushers" in the situation? Who wants to keep things quiet?
> Does it pass the Mom Test: Would you tell her? Would she do it?
> Does it pass the TV Test: Would you tell a nationwide audience?
> Does it pass the Market Test: Could you advertise the activity to gain a market edge?

2. Does your instinct tell you that something is wrong?
> Does it pass the Smell Test: Does the situation "smell"?

Formal Guidelines

1. Does the act violate corporate policy?
2. Does the act violate corporate or professional codes of conduct or ethics?
3. Does the act violate the Golden Rule?

Ethical Principles

Rights and Duties (deontology)

Are any rights abridged?
> The right to know
> The right to privacy
> The right to property

Are any duties or responsibilities not met?

Personal duties:
- Trust
- Integrity
- Truthfulness
- Gratitude and reparation
- Justice
- Beneficence and nonmaleficence
- Self-improvement

Professional duties (responsibilities)
> For all professionals:
>> Maintain appropriate professional relationships
>> Maintain efficacy
> For information professionals in particular:
>> Maintain confidentiality
>> Maintain impartiality

Consequentialism (teleology)

Does the action minimize actual and potential harm?

> Egoism: good for me, least harm to me
> Utilitarianism: good for the group, least harm for the group
> Altruism: good for all, some harm to me

Kant's Categorical Imperative

The principle of consistency: What if everyone acted this way?
The principle of respect: Are people treated as ends rather than means?

Step II. Isolating the major ethical dilemma What is the ethical dilemma to be resolved NOW? State it using the form: Should **someone** do or not do **something**? (Repeated from page 1.)

_____

_____

_____

Step III. Analyzing the ethicality of both alternatives in Step II

Consequentialism

   A. If action in Step II is done, who, if anyone, will be harmed? _____

   B. If action in Step II is not done, who, if anyone, will be harmed? _____

   C. Which alternative results in the least harm, A or B? [ ] A   [ ] B

   D. If action in Step II is done, who, if anyone, will benefit?   _____

   E. If action in Step II is not done, who, if anyone, will benefit? _____

   F. Which alternative results in the maximum benefit, D or E? [ ] D   [ ] E

Rights and Duties

   G. What **rights** have been or may be abridged? What **duties** have been or may be neglected? Identify the stakeholder and the right or duty. When listing a right, show its corresponding duty and vice versa.

_____

_____

_____

_____

_____

Kant's Categorical Imperative

   H. If action in Step II is done, who, if anyone, will be treated with *dis*respect? _____

   I. If action in Step II is not done, who, if anyone, will be treated with *dis*respect? _____

   J. Which alternative is preferable, H or I? [ ] H   [ ] I

   K. If action in Step II is done, who, if anyone, will be treated *un*like others? _____

   L. If action in Step II is not done, who, if anyone will be treated *un*like others? _____

   M. Which alternative is preferable, K or L? [ ] K   [ ] L

   N. Are there benefits if everyone did action in Step II? _____

   O. Are there benefits if nobody did action in Step II? _____

   P. Which alternative is preferable, N or O? [ ] N   [ ] O

Step IV. Making a decision and planning the implementation

A. Make a defensible ethical decision.

Based on the analysis in Step III, answer the question in Step II. Indicate the letters of the categories that best support your response. Add any arguments justifying your choice of these ethical principles to support your decision. Where there are conflicting rights and duties, choose and defend those that take precedence. (Note: Just make and justify your choice here; leave any action steps for parts B and D below.)

_____
_____
_____

B. List the specific steps needed to implement your defensible ethical decision.

_____
_____
_____
_____
_____
_____

C. Show how the major stakeholders are affected by these actions.

_____
_____
_____
_____
_____

D. What other longer-term changes (political, legal, technical, societal, organizational) would help prevent such problems in the future?

_____
_____
_____
_____
_____

E. What should have been done or not done in the first place (at the pivot point) to avoid this dilemma?

_____
_____
_____
_____

Name _____ Class _____ Date _____ Case # _____

A FOUR-STEP ANALYSIS PROCESS

The legal assessment and application of guidelines have helped you to discover that something in this situation requires a closer look. Using this worksheet carry out each step of the analysis process to resolve the ethical dilemma. Refer to the explanation in Chapter 3 for details.

Step I. Understanding the situation

A. List and number the relevant facts.

Number   *Fact*

_____   _____

_____   _____

_____   _____

_____   _____

_____   _____

_____   _____

_____   _____

_____   _____

B. Which of these raises an ethical issue? Why? What is the potential or resulting harm?

Fact (number)   *Potential or resulting harm*

[__]   _____

[__]   _____

[__]   _____

[__]   _____

[__]   _____

C. List the stakeholders involved.

_____

_____

_____

_____

Step II. Isolating the major ethical dilemma

What is the ethical dilemma to be resolved NOW?

State it using the form: Should **someone** do or not do **something**? Note: Just state the dilemma here; leave any reasoning for Step III.

_____

_____

_____

Figure 3-1
Approaches to Ethical Decision Making

Law and Ethics

Does the law provide an answer? (Professional help should be sought.)

Guidelines

Informal Guidelines

1. Is there something you or others would prefer to keep quiet?
   Are there "shushers" in the situation? Who wants to keep things quiet?
   Does it pass the Mom Test: Would you tell her? Would she do it?
   Does it pass the TV Test: Would you tell a nationwide audience?
   Does it pass the Market Test: Could you advertise the activity to gain a market edge?

2. Does your instinct tell you that something is wrong?
   Does it pass the Smell Test: Does the situation "smell"?

Formal Guidelines

1. Does the act violate corporate policy?
2. Does the act violate corporate or professional codes of conduct or ethics?
3. Does the act violate the Golden Rule?

Ethical Principles

Rights and Duties (deontology)

Are any rights abridged?
   The right to know
   The right to privacy
   The right to property

Are any duties or responsibilities not met?

Personal duties:
   - Trust
   - Integrity
   - Truthfulness
   - Gratitude and reparation
   - Justice
   - Beneficence and nonmaleficence
   - Self-improvement

Professional duties (responsibilities)
   For all professionals:
      Maintain appropriate professional relationships
      Maintain efficacy
   For information professionals in particular:
      Maintain confidentiality
      Maintain impartiality

Consequentialism (teleology)

Does the action minimize actual and potential harm?

   Egoism: good for me, least harm to me
   Utilitarianism: good for the group, least harm for the group
   Altruism: good for all, some harm to me

Kant's Categorical Imperative

The principle of consistency: What if everyone acted this way?
The principle of respect: Are people treated as ends rather than means?

Step II. Isolating the major ethical dilemma What is the ethical dilemma to be resolved NOW? State it using the form: Should **someone** do or not do **something**? (Repeated from page 1.)

_____

_____

_____

Step III. Analyzing the ethicality of both alternatives in Step II

Consequentialism

A. If action in Step II is done, who, if anyone, will be harmed? _____

B. If action in Step II is not done, who, if anyone, will be harmed? _____

C. Which alternative results in the least harm, A or B? [ ] A   [ ] B

D. If action in Step II is done, who, if anyone, will benefit?   _____

E. If action in Step II is not done, who, if anyone, will benefit? _____

F. Which alternative results in the maximum benefit, D or E? [ ] D   [ ] E

Rights and Duties

G. What **rights** have been or may be abridged? What **duties** have been or may be neglected? Identify the stakeholder and the right or duty. When listing a right, show its corresponding duty and vice versa.

_____

_____

_____

_____

_____

Kant's Categorical Imperative

H. If action in Step II is done, who, if anyone, will be treated with *dis*respect? _____

I. If action in Step II is not done, who, if anyone, will be treated with *dis*respect? _____

J. Which alternative is preferable, H or I? [ ] H   [ ] I

K. If action in Step II is done, who, if anyone, will be treated *un*like others? _____

L. If action in Step II is not done, who, if anyone will be treated *un*like others? _____

M. Which alternative is preferable, K or L? [ ] K   [ ] L

N. Are there benefits if everyone did action in Step II? _____

O. Are there benefits if nobody did action in Step II? _____

P. Which alternative is preferable, N or O? [ ] N   [ ] O

Step IV. Making a decision and planning the implementation

A. Make a defensible ethical decision.

Based on the analysis in Step III, answer the question in Step II. Indicate the letters of the categories that best support your response. Add any arguments justifying your choice of these ethical principles to support your decision. Where there are conflicting rights and duties, choose and defend those that take precedence. (Note: Just make and justify your choice here; leave any action steps for parts B and D below.)

_____

_____

_____

B. List the specific steps needed to implement your defensible ethical decision.

_____

_____

_____

_____

_____

_____

C. Show how the major stakeholders are affected by these actions.

_____

_____

_____

_____

_____

D. What other longer-term changes (political, legal, technical, societal, organizational) would help prevent such problems in the future?

_____

_____

_____

_____

E. What should have been done or not done in the first place (at the pivot point) to avoid this dilemma?

_____

_____

_____

_____

Index